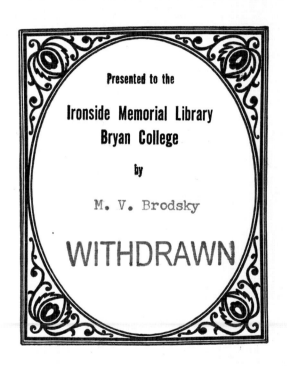

17-18

rowded

CP

ews

and lonely people

CROWDED PEWS AND LONELY PEOPLE

Marion Leach Jacobsen

TYNDALE HOUSE PUBLISHERS
Wheaton, Illinois

Coverdale House Publishers Ltd.
London, England

Dedicated lovingly
to all the members of your church,
who need each other
so much

Crowded Pews and Lonely People
Originally published under the title *Saints and Snobs*

Library of Congress Catalog Card Number 72-78876
ISNB 8423-0475-4, paper

First printing, July 1975

Printed in the United States of America

CONTENTS

—Accepting yourself—Liking yourself—Your best self—
Test yourself—Positive and negative characteristics—God
can change you.

body — Be available — Enjoy life — Single adults — Wait — Expect.

INTRODUCTION

This Book and You

This book is about *you*—if you're a follower of Jesus Christ and associated in any group with other Christians. Whether you are a happy, well-accepted member of that group or a less well-accepted, lonely person needing friends, this book is for *you*.

All Christians agree that God's people should be friendly, loving and compassionate, and multitudes of His people are. Potentially there is no fellowship on earth so sweet and so satisfying as the fellowship of men and women who are genuinely committed to Jesus Christ. If individuals and groups in the Christian community sometimes fall short of this potential, the resulting problems cannot be solved by denying that they exist.

This book undertakes to deal lovingly and biblically with those problems. It doesn't speak in vague generalities but is frankly realistic. It is, however, positive, not negative, and relates human lack and failure to the wonderful plan and power of God for good relations among His people.

Let's start with the assumption that God wants Christians to find in their local churches the personal acceptance, friends, love, and practical care they need. Because this is His ideal it becomes our objective. But let's also be honest enough to admit that not everyone finds this deep need met in the local church.

Christian love is a subject that has been handled in many books and sermons, but few deal with the nitty-gritty of personal relationships where problems arise within the family of Jesus Christ.

What I have to say is the result of my own experience and the experiences of many others. For fourteen years I was assistant to the pastor of a large church, teacher of many adult classes, and sponsor of youth groups. Since then I have been a member of several churches in different parts of the country. During these years, for some unknown reason, people have made a practice of telling me their troubles. The accumulation of these experiences, plus a strong compulsion which I believe is from God, have made it impossible for me not to write this book.

It will not survey all the personal problems of individual Christians or the churches to which they belong. It is concerned with a specific, restricted area—how to make acceptance, love, and friendship available in local groups of believers.

To read only parts of this book can give a false impression of its true position and message. Every part must be seen in the light of the rest.

I want to acknowledge gratefully the excellent material of the publishers and writers mentioned in the footnotes; the strong support and professional help of my editor-husband; and the countless friends whose enthusiasm and openness have encouraged me and contributed largely to the writing of this book. Also the loyal and capable assistance of my typist and friend, Mary Guymon DeGroff.

1

THE POTENTIAL AND
THE PROBLEM

"But we won't know what to expect at this church," Karen Bailey said uneasily to her husband, Bill. "If it was just our own denomination we'd still be strangers but we'd at least know how they do things."

"I know," Bill told her sympathetically, "but let's give it a try. It's practically across the street from us and lots of people go there. They all look happy and friendly when they come out. And remember it's almost five miles across the city to First Church. With our three kids we'd be doing *some* taxiing getting them to that church for their different age-group meetings, and picking them up afterwards.

"If we don't like this church across the street when we visit it tomorrow," he added, "I promise: we'll try First Church next Sunday."

Bill and Karen had come from Connecticut to a Kansas City suburb and were finding the adjustments difficult. They missed the relatives and friends they had left behind, and their new neighbors largely ignored them.

Six-year-old Steve had been invited to Sunday school at the nearby church by Pete, a boy in his class in school, and was eager to go. But his mother was not optimistic as she and her family crossed the street next morning. She was a shy woman and shrank from meeting new people and unfamiliar situations.

11

"We're the Baileys," her husband announced to the smiling man at the door of the church. "Can you tell us where we'll find the classes for our children? They're six, nine, and eleven years old."

"Certainly," was the cordial response. "I'm Bob Hanson and we're glad you're here. It's a little complicated finding the rooms in our new education building, so why don't you let me take the children to their classes, introduce them to their teachers, and then pick them up afterwards and bring them back here to meet you?

"This is my wife Barbara," he added, introducing them to her. "She'll be glad to take you two with her to the Berean Class, and I'll see you there later."

Karen and Bill exchanged smiles of relief. The initial crisis, at least, was over.

At the dinner table that noon, the Bailey family reviewed the experiences of the morning.

"Pete sat with me and let me look on his Bible," Steve informed them happily.

"The girls in my class didn't talk to me," Linda admitted, "but the teacher invited me to a party the class is having at her house Friday."

Bud reported, "There was a guy in my class who went to Connecticut for his vacation last summer. They call him 'Red,' and he said he'd ride over on his bike after school tomorrow.

"Did you like this church, Mom?" he added hopefully.

"Why, yes." His mother's warmth surprised them all. "It wasn't as hard as I was afraid it would be. Everyone was friendly and seemed interested in us. I'd like to go again next Sunday."

"The pastor said he'd call on us this week," Bill added, "which of course is usual. But we met lots of other folks and the Hansons asked us over for coffee tonight."

The Baileys had found a new church home. They grew to love it, and often reminisced about the more or less insignificant details that had made up their impressions of the crucial first visit — the people who were friendly, helpful, and open-hearted.

But realistically we know that many who cross the threshholds of our churches do not leave with such satisfying first impressions. Some wisely come back, reach out to people rather than waiting to be welcomed, and eventually discover that their original unfavorable impressions weren't correct.

I shall never forget a Sunday in a Phoenix church when the pastor preached an unusually short sermon about Christian fellowship and then opened the service to testimonies (some prearranged) from newer members of the congregation. At least half a dozen people stood and told in some detail their early experiences in coming to that church. They named individuals who had greeted them warmly, introduced them to others, followed up with telephone calls, personal visits, and invitations to their homes.

Little acts of helpfulness had loomed large. One woman had offered to hold a baby while a visiting mother attended to an older child. Someone had asked a new couple to sit with them at their first service. A family with several children had invited a new family to bring their children to a desert picnic. A Junior High boy had offered to pick up a new Sunday school visitor on his way to Boy's Brigade the following week. A neighbor had brought in a pot of soup when a mother, new in the congregation, had become ill.

The simplicity of these small kindnesses stood out in contrast to the significant part they had played in the process of the church's welcoming and assimilating these new people. And conspicuous in the recital were the names of the individuals who had been available to God for this inconspicuous and often unsung service.

Are you available to Him and to needy people (new or old) in your church?

Why Go To Church?

Why does a person go to church? He chooses one church of many, makes his way there, sits down in a pew. Why has he come?

There are many reasons. It may simply make him feel good — nicely religious and respectable. Or he may be trying to fill up an emptiness that he feels, a longing to find meaning to life. He may have personal problems and hope that he will get help — some solution to his situation. Or he may just be looking for profitable business or professional contacts. If he is a real Christian, he is probably looking for Bible teaching and preaching, and wants to worship God.

But it is safe to say that whatever other motives brought him to church, down underneath — consciously or unconsciously — he also came to be with people, to be part of a group, to find fellowship with other human beings, to make friends.

Seated in his pew, which may be full, he is surrounded by people, but as he leaves the church, no matter how the sermon or music may have impressed him, he leaves with definite feelings either of having made warm touch with his fellow-worshipers or of having been among many and yet somehow alone.

A keen observer of the human scene has remarked that a person's first twelve minutes in a church determines whether or not he will come back. It is a solemn thought that not only his return to church but, if he happens not to be a Christian, eventually his eternal salvation may also hang in the balance.

In Christ God offers man the meeting of his most desperate need — forgiveness of sin, escape from its fearful penalty, adoption as a child of God, resources adequate for any circumstance life may bring, and the certainty of heaven. This great salvation and destiny seem almost too good to be true, but they are real and the Christian church may well glory in the message it proclaims.

But in the glow of proclaiming it, we may overlook what the New Testament makes equally clear — that God's planning includes the experience of warm, satisfying, productive personal relationships among His people.

They are to accept one another unconditionally, to love one another warmly and loyally in spite of personal faults and failures, and without discrimination.

Unfriendliness and snobbishness — cliquishness among adults, and exclusiveness among youth — are not to be accepted as the normal pattern in people who claim to be personally related to Jesus Christ.

Of course the first concern of the Christian Church should be with man's greatest need — his need for God, for forgiveness of sin and for new life in Christ. But Christians should be as ready as any secular observer of the human scene to look squarely at *all* areas of personal need — especially those having to do with relationships among people. God has, as we shall see, many specific and practical things to say about them.

Embarrassing to Admit

On the surface it is easy to assume that all who have come into a personal experience with Jesus Christ have found instant joy, peace, and rightness in their relationship to God and to His people. Because we ourselves have developed some degree of Christian maturity, we may forget that many of God's people have not been delivered from self-centeredness and lovelessness. They are immature, not-yet-complete representatives of our Lord. But they are important to Him and should be included in our loving concern.

It may seem embarrassing to admit, after conversion, and especially after years of being identified with the Church, that anything is lacking either in one's own Christian experience or in the attitudes of supposedly model Christians who nevertheless seem unfriendly or indifferent.

How do you say to the people in your church, "Look, I'm lonely! I'm only half a couple, and I feel left out. My husband isn't a Christian and won't come to church with me, so I don't fit into the good fellowship enjoyed by couples here. I really need to find friends in my church."

Or, "Our son grew up in this church. But right now he's a gangly, insecure teen and the church kids won't have anything to do with him. He doesn't want to go to Sunday school or youth group any more because no one will sit with him or talk to him. He is so hurt and angry he says he'll show them he can find friends among the 'grease.' And that scares us."

Or, "I ride the same commuter trains morning and night, five days a week, month after month, but even though the other men from our church know who I am, they never sit with me or talk to me. I so need to share with someone the terrible pressure and anxiety I'm feeling over my job. I don't know how to handle the situation, and I'm not sure the pastor would understand this problem. I wonder if there's something about me that the men don't like, or are Christians just unfriendly?"

These samples represent the kind of grief some of God's children encounter, though usually they say nothing about it, and the *Ins* go on enjoying life either without noticing or caring that some are left out and feel rejected.

For practical purposes, let me define two terms here — the *Ins* and the *Outs*. These are rather shopworn labels but they are convenient and will enable me to avoid repeated definitions and qualifications. For my purposes, *Ins* are popular, well-accepted people. *Outs* are less well-accepted but not necessarily friendless or rejected. Many people belong somewhere between, but the categories are familiar and useful terms for this discussion.

Tertullian, one of the great Church fathers, wrote of the early Christians, "Behold how they love one another!" Their loving was distinctive — a kind of relationship that didn't generally exist among non-Christians. This rare, shining love crowns the fellowship of many Christians today, but others have not found it in their church experience.

Make no mistake, I fully recognize the presence and power of genuine Christian love at work in the relationships of multitudes of modern Christians — love that is alive, artless, undiscriminating and all-inclusive, practical, overflowing, and endless. A host of Christians, including myself, know what it is to feel loved, cared for, and undergirded by the prayers and kindnesses of fellow Christians. Times of crisis — sickness or bereavement, for example — often increase our awareness of this loving interest and concern.

I would do the followers of Christ a terrible injustice if I gave the impression that most Christians are "a bunch of snobs," that the Church is just a lot of exclusive cliques, or that you have to be rich to belong to the *In* crowd there.

There is no community in all the world that has the dynamic available to the Church for accepting and loving people — including the unattractive and undeserving. If she sometimes fails to live up to this potential, blame thoughtless or selfish members, not the Christ who brought the Church into being and equipped her to become the most democratic, open-hearted, love-motivated community on the face of the earth.

Such love doesn't always conspicuously characterize Christian fellowship on the contemporary scene. To some, the Church represents a rich, satisfying experience, but to others it is to some degree disappointing, frustrating, or painful.

Many people are overwhelmed by the warm welcome and continuing love they receive at church. Others coming into the same group, looking for friends and a sense of belonging, may fail to find personal recognition and acceptance. They may even stop attending any church because of their disappointment. And we don't always know who was to blame — the misfit or the people who passed him by. Probably both.

A person who finds friends and a satisfying social life in one group of Christians may, after moving away, be unable to find friends and good social relationships in his new church home. I know two normally well-accepted couples who have experienced this disappointment in churches I would consider unusually friendly.

Plain Talk

Perhaps we give new converts the impression that the only reason God doesn't take them straight to heaven at once is so they can get busy and win others to Christ. This is surely part of His purpose, but only a part. We forget that developing each individual into an attractive, mature, loving member of the family of God is also an important phase of His purpose.

The new Christian needs clear understanding of his role in loving, supporting, encouraging, and cherishing his brothers and sisters in Christ. This is only one of his new responsibilities, but it is crucial to his own development and his function in the body of Christ. Yet we may be so preoccupied with his supporting the local church, attacking the economic and social ills of society, or even evangelizing the lost, according to the emphasis of our church or denomination, that we either ignore or accept as "human" the unlovelinesses and sins that disfigure him, spoil his relation to other believers, and damage the testimony of his church.

We ignore Mrs. A's problem — a tongue hung in the middle. She is an incessant dispenser of harmless and harmful information. This has permanently disqualified her from serving as chairman of one of the Women's Circles, but is accepted as "normal" for her.

Mr. B. needs to be delivered from a hot, uncontrolled temper that has cost him more than one job, is giving his wife ulcers, alienating his four children from the church and from Jesus Christ, and repeatedly stirring up fracases in the congregation.

"Buzz" Jones, 17, has such an unsanctified wit that he ridicules or mocks many a sensitive teen-ager right out of the youth group.

These are all attitudes that should be dealt with from the pulpit and in the Sunday school class, but, strangely enough, are usually not mentioned except in the vaguest generalities.

When God spoke to men through the Scriptures He didn't pretend that wrong attitudes were unknown among His followers. In both the Old and New Testaments, He gave repeated, specific, and vigorous attention to their shortcomings. He attacked lack of humility — pride and arrogance; hypocrisy — *saying* we care about others while doing nothing to meet their needs; the shame and danger of an uncontrolled tongue; injustice and taking advantage of the poor and underprivileged; greediness, and materialism; sexual immorality; and poor relationships at home. He wasn't so afraid of damaging His own image or hurting someone's feelings that He glossed over inconsistencies in His people. He spoke of them plainly. And He didn't assume that coming into a relationship with God would automatically correct and transform a life. He provides both the power and the pattern for change, but the individual has to *want* that change.

Please remember that this discussion revolves around personal relationships *within* a local group of believers. Someone will be sure to ask, "Aren't Christians supposed to be nice to people *outside* the church?" Of course they are. But *this* book is dealing with a limited subject — the need of every

Christian to find acceptance, friends, and love *in his local church,* and the responsibility of every other Christian to meet these needs.

As those who are committed followers of Jesus Christ learn to live lovingly with one another, they are conditioned to build good personal relationships with people outside their church. Later we will discuss more fully what *the church* can do to help solve social problems among its members, but let it be said here that one of the church's top priority responsibilities is to help individual Christians become like Jesus Christ — the kind of men and women God wants them to be. They need to know His pattern for everyday living and realize how He makes it possible for them to live that way.

Before Christians can accomplish much to solve the temporal or spiritual problems of the world, they must let God change them personally and reorder their relations to each other. Unchristlike attitudes and actions complicate and corrupt these relationships, and this corruption — lovelessness and disunity among Christians — repels the very people the Church should attract.

James Johnson, writing about the lack of a sense of community in the church, told about Larry, whom he had first known as a new Christian, "full of zeal and bouncing with the energy of new birth." Four years later he was still attending the church, "but something had gone out of him."

When asked to explain the situation, Larry was reluctant. "Well, I really don't know," he said, "I guess it's just that I've lost a sense of community among Christians. Or maybe I never had it . . . Maybe I'm just a rah-rah boy at heart — I don't know. I've been trying to pick out people in the church whom my wife and I could really call friends, the kind you can let your hair down with, the kind you'd find it easy to die for. What shocked us was not that we couldn't find that kind, but that actually there were only a few people out of 600 in that church with whom we even have a nodding acquaintance. . . . Sometimes I'd like to go talk to my old bartender friend of years back. . . . I had a thing going with Oscar in friendship that I haven't yet found in the church."[1]

Cover-up?

Church members like to think (and have others think) that loneliness, lovelessness, and snobbery don't exist among them. Those who vigorously defend the pure doctrines of the Bible and its way of life are reluctant to admit that in actual practice such social problems exist. They are more comfortable when everyone keeps his mask of spiritual pride and joy well in place instead of admitting that there is deep, humiliating hurt in the hearts of some of the church family.

This is a cover-up, *not for any lack in Christianity itself,* but for carelessness or snobbishness in some who wear the name Christian. We help no one by merely calling attention to these unfortunate inconsistencies, but we can't deal with the resulting problems in practical ways unless we first admit the real situation.

The same God who instituted marriage instituted the Church, and used each to illustrate truth about the other. What do we do when we find flaws and failures in married life? Condemn the institution of marriage? Or deal frankly with the problems that make it, in actual practice, less than what God means it to be?

And what shall we do about the flaws and failures that creep into relations among Christians? Condemn Christianity or the Church? Or face the problems honestly and look for constructive, God-given solutions?

The New Testament gives a complete pattern for good interpersonal relationships among Christians, but some of us have either lost sight of it or lost the incentive and dynamic for living it.

Outsiders are quick to observe among Christians inconsistent attitudes and actions that violate that beautiful God-given pattern. We give the cold shoulder to people of a different race or of humble circumstances. Personal quarrels leak out. One member hasn't spoken to another for six months. A young person making an effort to be assimilated into the church youth group, feels rejected and leaves. Large contributors are reported to enjoy special privileges and influence.

Christians who are reluctant to admit that there is discrimination among them, that anyone in their congregation is exclusive or excluded, may label any concern over problems of social acceptance as "self-centered," "carnal," "worldly," and "unspiritual." To talk about such problems, they feel, reflects on the church and her Lord. They try to protect Christianity by denying, ignoring, or concealing these defects in Christian fellowship. They overlook the fact that because discrimination, as well as inability to accept oneself and one's circumstances, are out of keeping with the Christian way of life, such social problems should be squarely faced — not ignored or hidden.

I circulated about seventy-five brief questionnaires, related to this area of need, in two adult Sunday school classes, inviting members to share their experiences anonymously. I asked:

1. Give specific instances of times when you felt warmly and personally loved and cared for in the church family — how Christians befriended you when you were new in the group, sick, in trouble, or lonely.

2. What is your evaluation of large and small group fellowship among Christians?

3. What problems have you faced in the church — loneliness, lack of personal friends, a feeling of not being included? Have your children felt unaccepted in the youth group? Why do you think people ignored or rejected you? For what good reasons (and there are some) have you not included some people in your social life?

4. What suggestions would you make if you were writing in this area? What should Christians do or not do to find friends? To help others find friends?

5. What has God meant to you in your social relationships with other Christians?

Just to demonstrate what a hush-hush surrounds the discussion of such matters (and I realize they *are* personal), let me tell you that I received only three replies. One was frank, vigorous, beautifully honest, and practically helpful.

Another was as follows (spelling corrected): "I think you have no right to ask these questions. They are matters which belong between a Christian and Christ. The response you get will not be accurate — and your answers will fall into two general categories: (1) filled with pride (2) overflowing with problems. Hope you will stop before hurting too many people — and write something worthwhile. This is the kind of stuff the liberals love — always learning but never coming to the knowledge of the truth."

I humbly commend to my anonymous friend that I am undertaking to help people who have *already* been "hurt." I am writing because some Christians *are* "filled with pride" and many others *are* "overflowing with problems." Perhaps both need a gentle reminder that God is not indifferent to either condition. As for learning and never arriving at proper conclusions, many highly privileged Christians seem to have done a lot of so-called "learning" without ever coming to that knowledge of God's truth that changes and sets in order one's personal relationships.

I don't so much want to rebuke as to encourage and constructively help all Christians, who should be deeply involved in each other's needs.

In a nation-wide survey which I also conducted among churches of many different denominations, one member contended that one's relation to God is the only thing that matters, and that when the vertical relation (i.e., to God) is what it should be, the horizontal (one's relation to others) will take care of itself. There is much truth in this claim, but if wrong relationships on the human level reveal some basic fault in one's relation to God, then by all means let's recognize, not camouflage, our failure toward others and reexamine the quality — or even the reality — of our relation to a God who abhors arrogance, self-seeking, discrimination, lack of compassion and mercy, jealousy, false humility, self-pity, and a holier-than-thou attitude.

It's *not* unspiritual to admit honestly your own need for the love and the friendship of other Christians, or frankly to examine yourself and your ability to make contact with those with whom you should have most in common in Christ.

It's easy to blame acquaintances who bypass you, but it takes courage to look honestly at yourself and the impression you make on others. This book will undertake to help you do just that.

Neither is it unspiritual to remind Christians who have found a better than average adjustment in the Christian community that they are still necessarily involved in this problem by their contacts with people who do have real and unmet social needs. You may hardly be aware of these needs if your own life is filled with satisfying human relationships. You have personal qualities and a life situation that have opened to you doors of acceptance and social privilege that many people never know. You may hardly understand what I'm writing about, because social exclusion never happened to you.

But if, as a Christian, you have any genuine concern for the problems other believers face, you'll try to comprehend what it means to be left out, to be disappointed because people are not drawn to you, or because you don't have places to go socially and friends to go with.

You try to understand and meet the needs of people who face problems caused by blindness, racial discrimination, poverty, physical injury or disease, bereavement, or religious persecution. You reach out to them in sympathy and love, and offer what practical help you can. But what is your attitude toward socially needy Christians in your own immediate world who, for one reason or another, are not numbered among your personal friends? What can you be or do for *them?*

Because the less well-accepted individual is acutely sensitive to his personal need, I have more to say to and about him. But his need can never be fully met unless you Christians who are more socially secure are also open to what God has to say to *you.*

Some Like It Cool

In undertaking a discussion of social relationships among members of a local church group, I realize that some people relate to the church of their choice only by attending it on Sunday and by making use, on appropriate occasions, of its special services—baptism, Communion, confirmation, marriage, funerals. They have little or no personal contact with individuals in their church and would agree with one distinguished Christian who said to me, "I like it that way."

To such people, any discussion of interpersonal relationships among members of a church group may be a matter of complete indifference. Their social contacts are rooted largely in their broader family ties or in their neighborhoods, or grow out of business contacts or the organizations to which they belong outside the church. They come to church on Sunday to worship and receive instruction. They go home and come back a week later without any in-between contacts with their fellow worshipers.

This may be a practical arrangement, space- and time-wise, but it represents a serious loss on both sides of the ledger. Every Christian should be happily profiting through personal contacts with other members of his church, and be contributing to the meeting of their needs. It's possible and delightful to have good friends outside of one's own church family, but such friends don't completely take the place of good personal relationships on the inside.

Where It Hurts

Probably women and young people feel the most social unease. Women who stay at home are largely shut up to the house, the children, and near neighbors. Almost every morning, their husbands step out into a colorful and exciting (be it ever so strenuous) world, meeting people and adventures of various kinds. They enjoy returning to the seclusion of home, but the little woman may long to get away, to meet people, to taste life in a wider dimension.

Being a woman, I have had other women share heartaches and longings with me — their hunger for fellowship, their failure to be accepted in their church group, to feel that they belong to a circle of close Christian friends. But it was a man who sent his wife to me to pour out the burden of both their hearts because of the social rejection they were experiencing. I shall never forget my amazement when this delightful woman, who had been active in a thriving Evangelical church for years, said simply, "We just don't have any friends."

Women also feel the pressure of social problems because they are largely responsible for the social life of the family — for keeping up with old friends, making new ones, and entertaining guests. They must furnish and keep in order the home to which friends come; they plan, prepare, and serve meals and refreshments for guests. Women are especially sensitive to lack of success in this area.

The mother is usually closest to her children's social problems too, whether they revolve around church, school and neighborhood situations, or the complications of wider adolescent relationships. She probably feels it more strongly than her husband when their children are excluded or just left out of other children's activities.

A. B. Hollingshead, writing about churches in the so-called Bible Belt, says that many of the youngsters who attend church functions regularly carry their status feelings with them, often in a most unchristian manner. He tells of one select gang of girls attending the Sunday Night "Fellowship Meetings"(!) of the most elite church in Elmtown, who "deliberately make any girl of whom they do not approve feel so uncomfortable" that she will not attend again.[2]

Adults may at least keep underground their antipathies toward each other, but children and young people are not so subtle in their rejection and persecution of certain of their peers, even in Christian schools and churches.

Especially at the elementary and junior high level they often openly enjoy excluding certain individuals from their more intimate groups, and may make a project of humiliating and tormenting someone they decide to ostracize. Refusing to sit next to the outcast, whispering about him, or openly passing out invitations to parties to which he is not invited are representative of their torture tools.

One of the *Ins,* not content to display his own superiority, may marshall his friends and get them in on the act, swelling their own egos as they watch the embarrassment and disintegration of the object of their ridicule.

If you'd like to document the existence of such attitudes, talk to the right children in almost any school room or Sunday school department, or, better still, talk to parents who share such a child's agony.

Teachers and other leaders are not always compassionate in handling these situations. One Christian elementary school gym teacher, every week, month after month, had two class captains choose sides, calling out names, one at a time. And the same two uncoordinated children always suffered the humiliation of being chosen last.

In many instances, the same few outstanding members of a class or youth group hold all the offices and are given the prominent parts in any performance. Even if, in such a situation, a compassionate teacher or leader were to assign a coveted responsibility to an unpopular person, the *In* crowd might see to it that no one cooperated. So usually such choices are made by popular election, which insures the success of the project — and the perpetuation of leadership by the *Ins*.

A couple who worked with high school young people in a liberal church were dismayed at the unmerciful snobbishness and cliquishness exhibited among them, and believed it was probably because their charges' parents had not taught the Bible to their children at home.

Later, however, when this couple became involved in an outstandingly conservative church they were appalled to discover that these young people, who *had* been raised by thoroughly evangelical parents, were no different in their attitudes toward one another.

Had these parents failed to teach biblical attitudes to their children? Or had they failed to set an example in their own social relationships? Or are secular influences outside the home today so strong that young people relate to each other according to non-Christian rather than Christian patterns?

Unpopularity, like popularity, is often deserved, as we shall see. But deserved or undeserved, such painful situations are conspicuously out of place among Christians. We must remember, though, that children and young people are human beings as well as representatives of the Christian culture. They will come into personal and spiritual maturity (as most of their elders did) by a gradual, usually lengthy process. This development may be as slow as physical maturing (or slower!). Meantime, many suffer.

Nearly all my nationally surveyed church members felt a book should be written about this problem, and one high school fellow felt the need was so great that I should write *two* — one for young people and one for adults!

About half reported having felt lack of acceptance at some stage of their years in school, or having been mocked and called painful names as a child, or having not been allowed to be a part of certain play groups, or now having children of their own who feel unaccepted by their peers.

Some children experience rejection because of their own shyness, bossiness, unbearable meanness, or lack of physical skills. Others don't fit in because they are "different" — slower (or too quick!) to learn, or somehow physically out-of-the-ordinary, or more interested in books and ideas, or more creative in ways that seem strange to other youngsters.

Parents' attitudes may cut their children off from neighborhood playmates. Perhaps parents interfere too often with the children's play, or (more disastrously) with their squabbles. Perhaps they fail to provide their children with needed play equipment — skates, yard swings, a sandbox, tent, or bicycle. Or they may be too protective about their lawn and plantings, or their house and its furnishings, or careless about their relations with the parents of their children's playmates.

I know of two families who even prohibited their children from playing with any neighbor children who didn't belong to Christian families of their own particular religious variety!

Believe it or not, most teen-agers, no matter how *In* they may be, feel considerable tension over their status among their peers. Many Christian young people, because of spiritual immaturity (or often because they're actually "Christian" in name only), have attitudes and act toward each other in ways that are displeasing to God as well as painful to one another.

Few adults, unless they have worked with this age group or are among those rare parents whose teens communicate freely with them, realize what goes on in the personal relationships of young people today. Teens are too often more human than Christian — self-centered, critical, unmercifully cruel to each other; feasting on gossip (listen to one end of one of their 30-minute telephone conversations!), and resorting for personal advantage to lying and malicious misrepresentation of what others say and do.

I personally know young people who have afterwards admitted that the juicy morsel (sometimes a *large* "morsel") that they told was just "for fun" and that there was not a speck of truth in it. They laugh about it, but sometimes the damage done can never be repaired.

"A man who is caught lying to his neighbor and says, 'I was just fooling,' is like a madman throwing around firebrands, arrows and death!"[3]

Even in churches that are sound in doctrine and evangelical in practice, a certain dominating group of young people (sometimes *one member* of it) may decide not only who shall be admitted to the clique but who shall be dropped or excluded. If one member of the inner circle dares to "be friends" with someone outside the group, he risks being dropped by the gang.

One mother told me how she and her husband had tried to encourage their son to be friendly to church young people outside of the small group of special friends he was so enjoying. He did try, she told me, but would go just so far and then withdraw. I was pretty sure why. If he had made any firm friendships outside of that *In* bunch, he himself could very well have become an *"out*sider."

Many who read this — perhaps the older folks — may think that I'm unfair to our Christian young people, and it's true that all youth don't fall into this pattern. But those who know the situation at firsthand — including a multitude of teens themselves — will confirm what I say. To some degree, the situation has always been so, but I believe it is more acute today.

That this problem is real and pressing even in Christian colleges is evidenced by the request of a group of concerned students on a midwest campus for a chapel program on loneliness. The result was three consecutive chapels — student-planned — devoted to the presentation of this problem as it exists on a *Christian* college campus. Hundreds of students share dormitories and classrooms, pass each other on campus walks, and are present together at countless extracurricular activities, but many somehow hardly make touch with each other. Many find college life exhilarating and fulfilling, but others feel lost and lonely, overlooked if not rejected, and see themselves as failures in the arena of human relations.

Unless we help such young people to find a niche on their own level, they are likely to become critical, bitter, "a searcher for scapegoats" on whom to blame their misfortunes.[4] And Eric Hoffer agrees with Vance Packard that such misfits are "easy recruits for almost any leader who promises to set up a completely new social order." They become "potential candidates for mass movements."

Well-accepted and popular young people, as well as the misfits, often sense the lack of real Christian love among the members of their church group. Though they may be party to the wrong attitudes that create this lovelessness, they know down deep that they haven't found in their church the kind of unique love Christianity promises and every heart longs for. Even self-centered popularity is a poor substitute for genuine Christian love.

After a winter youth retreat sponsored by a well-known church, the young people were asked by their leader for their reactions to the four days they had spent together away from their normal environment. One member startled the group by saying, "I was impressed by the fact that there was no love in our group." Competition, self-interest, harsh judging, gossip, cliquishness, and snobbery hadn't been hard to find.

When disenchanted with the church as they find it today, young people are turning in surprising numbers to other groups (e.g., the Jesus People) that offer acceptance, a sort of oneness, the love they failed to find in their local churches.

Some turn to charismatic groups that, however off balance or unscriptural they may or may not be, often provide a warmer, less formal kind of fellowship that gives the individual worshiper a feeling of being an integral part of the group, accepted and loved.

One thriving but eccentric charismatic group is reputed to be the haven of social rejects from other Christian communities. I asked one member if it was the fellowship there that had attracted her. She thought for a moment and then replied, "Not fellowship so much as oneness." I had visited her group and could understand what she meant.

Some young church-goers have gone completely outside the Christian structure, rejecting not only the Church and Christianity but the entire social and economic establishment. At Woodstock, or Fort Lauderdale, or San Francisco, or countless other locales, the Flower Children identified with a welcoming mass of kindred seekers and rebels who offered them what they hadn't found in their homes or churches — a kind of love that seemed to bind them together.

Let me add this: Wherever — in church or school — the love of Christ *has* possessed a group of Christians its members will never forget what they have experienced there — total acceptance, honest sharing, and genuine loving; a happiness that is overflowing, and a fellowship to which they can invite outsiders, knowing that when they come they will see the reality of Christ's love lived out in His children.

Such fellowship is rather rare even in places where you'd expect to find it. And sometimes it turns up in most unlikely places. But, if you can't find it, you can help make it!

2

CHRISTIANS ARE PEOPLE TOO

Christians are human beings! Before we can think realistically about their social needs, we must remember that even though they differ from non-Christians in important ways because of their relation to God, they are quite like them in others.

Let's think about two in particular.

First, like the rest of the human race, they have certain basic needs. And second, they are part of a society that, in any culture, becomes more or less layered or "stratified" — divided into groups of people who are considered, or consider themselves, to be either above or below other groups. Both this universal need and the stratification of society in general bear directly on the social problems Christians face in their relations with each other.

Since Christians are also human beings, they share the basic need to love and to be loved, a need for recognition, security, challenge, new experiences, achievement. This makes personal fulfilment in life practically impossible without satisfying relations with other people.

It's true that God, in the last analysis, is the only indispensable factor in the life of a Christian. When a man is in the most dire and unlikely circumstances, utterly cut off from any human relationships, God can meet all his essential needs. But

31

it is also true that He made us to live, normally, among other human beings. Someone has put it, "You can't be a Christian alone."

William Glasser, in his bold and convincing *Reality Therapy*, declares, "At all times in our lives we must have at least one person who cares about us and whom we care for ourselves. If we do not have this . . . we will not be able to fulfill our basic needs." Among these basic needs, he points out, are "the need to love and to be loved and the need to feel that we are worthwhile to ourselves and to others."

So your need to be personally accepted by others, and closely related to some, isn't just to spare you the shame of rejection but to make possible the high fulfilment for which God designed you. Without these satisfactory relationships with others, your basic individual needs won't be fulfilled on the human level.

It's a scientifically demonstrated fact that even an infant who is given the most ideal physical care doesn't develop normally if the ingredient of love is missing.

Such lack over a period of years can produce severe frustration and has, in rare cases, led to suicide — even within a church group!

Wanting acceptance and friends isn't only normal, it's *important*. It is in such relationships (in the home or outside it) that we grow and share as persons. Some people think that when we have found a new and good relation to God, we don't need anyone else — that if we're truly "spiritual" we won't be concerned about being accepted by people, about having friends. Let me ask these folks a question: Did you ever hear of anyone getting to be so spiritual that he didn't any longer need food, or air, or exercise, or sleep? Neither does one become so spiritual that human relationships are meaningless, unimportant, or unnecessary. Rather, they take on greater meaning and value in the Christian family.

The Apostle James wrote sharply to first-century Christians who only pretended to be concerned about the needs of fellow Christians: "Suppose there are brothers and sisters who need . . . and don't have enough. . . . What good is there in your saying to them, 'God bless you!' . . . if you don't give them the necessities of life?"[1] Knowing that others care about you *is a necessity of life.* So genuine loving and caring for other Christians is an important part of our responsibility to them and to the God to whom we all belong.

Universal Loneliness

Everyone knows at times and to some degree what it means to feel alone. "Anyone who is sensitive to other persons realizes that there is an emotional aloneness, a homesickness of the soul, that is widespread."[2] Burkhart traces this malady to a number of sources — the movement of people from place to place; a world in "terrible travail . . . many merely existing"; children orphaned because of working parents or divorce; the vastness of the universe.

When Billy Graham is asked what problem plagues more people today than any other, he surprises most of his questioners by answering, "Loneliness." Paul Tournier labels this as "the most devastating malady of the age," and a distinguished physician says, "There is no human condition so acute — or so universal." Even in a crowd it is possible for one to feel this utter aloneness. And, as someone has observed, even marriage may not be a cure for essential loneliness; it may be, rather, companionship in loneliness.

The producers of a leading brand of coffee play upon this need for friends in advertising its product as: " . . . the taste that brings people together."

Christians not only experience this universal sort of aloneness, but may also feel isolated from others because of their allegiance to Jesus Christ. He frankly promised His followers that they wouldn't be popular with the world because of their relation to Him. They might also face rejection by their families and friends.

To some degree, this is true of Christians today who let it be known openly that they are committed to Christ. They may be ostracized by business associates, scorned by relatives, or ignored by individuals or groups in their particular world. Wherever it is experienced, this discrimination intensifies the

Christian's need for satisfying personal relationships within his own church or with individual Christians outside it.

One young woman of European background, since becoming a Christian, has been openly mocked, condemned, and personally rejected by the members of a club of nationals to which she has belonged for years. In extreme instances a young convert may be put out of his parents' home and disinherited because he has dared to go against his family's religious traditions.

New Christians may not only face exclusion by non-Christians, but may find it necessary by their own decision to break off some relationships or discontinue participation in some activities that they feel are not in line with their new Christian standards. This creates a greater need for new friendships and activities — needs that the Church should be prepared to meet.

Under these normal and abnormal pressures, a Christian reaches out to the members of his church group for acceptance, friendships, a sense of belonging.

Some never even have to reach. They are practically engulfed by welcoming attention. People not only greet them warmly but introduce them to other members of the congregation and invite them to their homes. Pastors call, invite them to join the church, and appoint them to offices and committees.

Others aren't so lucky. They are welcomed only by the appointed greeters. Though they attend the services and activities of the church regularly, and may be favored with a pastoral call, they wait patiently and optimistically to make friends and find some personal recognition that never comes. Perhaps no one intentionally snubs or ignores them, but for some reason they just "don't take." No one invites them home, or even talks long enough with them to get acquainted.

One attractive, intelligent, friendly couple said they had attended a reputedly friendly church, and even sung in the choir, for a whole lonely year before anyone showed them any personal friendship or invited them home. Perhaps they shouldn't have waited for others to make the first move.

In some instances, if the newcomer is judged an undesirable addition to the group (because of race, looks, dress, personality, position, or economic level), he may be tactfully discouraged by a variety of effective and subtle devices. If he leaves, well and good. If he stays, he learns his place — out on the chilly fringes of the charmed circle of church social life. This kind of performance is *not* characteristic of people who wear the name of Christ creditably, but unfortunately it is too often the practice of those who only wear the name.

Perhaps you're among the multitude of church members who have suffered from minor pricks and pains in your relation to others in the congregation — felt the sting of barbed remarks or the realization that someone who was usually cordial made a point of not seeing you as you passed. Or perhaps you entertained acquaintances in your home and they never invited you back. Or, when you faced unusual problems and pressures, those you thought were interested in you showed no concern. Some people are *too* sensitive to others' attitudes and too easily hurt, as we shall see later. But often hurts come not so much from a wounded person's being hypersensitive as from another's being insensitive, thoughtless, or even heartlessly cruel.

Have you ever been gradually or suddenly — but altogether — dropped by a friend or group of friends to whom you had been close for some time? Has this happened even though you knew of no reason for the break? This happens often enough in church circles for real or imagined reasons.

But don't forget that such unpleasant, disappointing experiences are not confined to Christian circles. Actually, there is probably *far less* of this thoughtlessness or snobbishness among the followers of Christ than elsewhere. However, loneliness and self-interest are also less excusable among Christians who profess to have adopted a whole new way of life.

The Status Seekers

It's impossible to talk about social pressures inside the Christian community without first taking a look at social stratification and status-seeking in general. Christians belong not only to their local circle of Christian contacts but also to a larger outside social structure that inevitably influences them. In the experience of a Christian, this outside pressure should be counteracted by the new life-focus he has found in Christ.

Many people enjoy life on their present social plateau and lose little sleep trying to reach another level. As Vance Packard observes, they "tend to accept a status hierarchy — and their place in it — naturally. Life is said to be more stable and serene in clearly stratified societies. . . . A society that encourages status-striving produces, in contrast, a good deal of bruising, disappointment, and ugly feelings."[3]

But, Packard points out, being restricted to the social and economic level into which you were born runs counter to the American ideal of equal opportunity. And if the pressing needs of our world are to be met, people from any level who have unusual potential should have the freedom to move ahead unhindered by class restrictions.

The craving for dominance or power — the urge to get ahead and on top — is said to be one of the most dynamic sources of human behavior, and is traced in part to a child's early feelings of inferiority in his relation to his parents and other adults in the family. Even in a Christian home, parents and their maturing child experience the conflict that develops as the youth tries to overcome his dependence and subjection and show himself and his world that he isn't actually inferior. In his great effort to demonstrate that he has outgrown childhood's necessary but temporary inferiority, he may exhibit frantic and unreasonable adolescent attitudes of superiority to his parents, his teachers, and his peers.

At this stage young people (even many who are Christians) are notoriously heartless and cruel to each other, driven by this desperate need to climb up from the underposition at home and achieve the highest possible level of acceptance and popularity among their classmates and friends. This adolescent struggle for status is normal and even valuable within limits, but when it is not controlled or outgrown it may develop into a life-long obsession to surpass and dominate others.

The Christian Church needs and is enriched by the leadership ability, as well as the financial support, of men who are ambitious, energetic, wise, and successful. But a church is sometimes riddled with problems that grow out of self-seeking determination to get ahead of others, to manipulate people, and to control the pastor as well as the members of the congregation.

Even the young church at Corinth was disrupted when its spiritual leaders became jealous of each other, bragged about themselves in order to boost their own image, and tried to discredit and degrade other leaders in the eyes of the congregation. Read in 2 Corinthians 11 (modern translation, please) about the Apostle Paul's anguish as he tries to undo the damage done to that local church by this ruthless scramble for position and power.

Parents may become infected with the "get ahead" virus, like the mother of the sons of Zebedee,[4] being overly ambitious for their children. They may try to maneuver their children's friendships, or unwisely (in some cases) insist on their children's having college educations in order to qualify for higher-level jobs and social status. They may even try to marry them off to someone from a higher economic or social level.

"To get ahead, to make good — these are the goals which are impressed on American children — to go someplace else, get on with it, count your success by the number you have passed on the road. . . . How can you tell a man is a success? Only by knowing how far he has come, how many he has bypassed, what he has in the way of power and possessions. What he is — as a person — is irrelevant, for to be a success is to have done something, rather than to have been a kind of person."[5]

How far removed this is from God's point of view!

Advertisers playfully refer to themselves as "merchants of discontent," and play no small part in increasing social and economic unrest, and infecting people with the itch for the position and possessions that spell status. One magazine advertisement urged: "Improve your ice cream with our coconut and attain social success overnight." Snob appeal spikes many ads. One proclaims a certain luxury car to be for "the person who can afford to be different."

Social Climbing

It is said that status is the great American dream. Too

many people are involved in a continual and gigantic struggle to rise to a higher social plane.

We Christians should be immune to the temptation to promote ourselves and get ahead of others, but unfortunately we too may be infected with that virus. All God's people need to take a clear look at the aggressive social climbing in American society and determine not to let it invade their relationships with each other.

"Social climbers" is the term used to describe those who try, with some success, to move upward and improve their social position. Someone has distinguished "social strainers" as those who make a great effort in that direction but have little success! What they strain for is simply beyond their reach.

Social climbing is a lonesome road. The one who tries to make his way into a social circle above his present level may injure himself as well as others in the climb. He must leave his present friends behind and at the same time take the risk that he may be regarded as an intruder by the group he wants to enter. So he may be entirely rejected.

Two precocious little girls in school were compelled to skip the second grade and were thrust into Grade Three. The friends they left behind resented their promotion, and so did their new classmates who had had to travel the longer route to their present eminence. For years the short-cutters wore the marks of this unfortunate "upward" move.

The social climber not only risks loneliness and rejection, but may lose his ability to make contact with people, to identify with them sincerely as human beings, to communicate with real interest. He *uses* people, eyeing them for what they can do for him, and accepting or rejecting them according to how well they fit into his determined effort to get on top. Someone well said, "The mark of a man is how he treats a person who can be of no possible use to him." Packard calls the climber a "lonely man making his way on a slippery slope."[6]

He may be unable to make friends in his higher social plateau because people sense his intense self-seeking and basic insincerity even though he tries to conceal it. As someone wisely put it, "It's usually easier to hide something than to hide the fact that you're hiding something."[7] The climber may also do serious damage to his own integrity as he climbs the social ladder without counting the cost to his conscience or to the well-being of others.

Even though allegiance to Jesus Christ and obedience to His teachings radically change a Christian's whole life perspective and should free him from this terrible urge to promote himself and dominate others, we need to remember that he still has a great need to feel personally accepted and loved.

Frustrated by Failure

There is often painful conflict between a person's goals and his ability to reach them. All are supposed to have equal opportunity to reach goals that attract them, but actually they don't. They may have been born handicapped by race, mentality, native talent, locality, or economic resources.[8]

In our more or less rigid society, Packard points out, millions of people find themselves settled into a fixed role in life, where there is no hope of change in status. Yet we keep on telling them that those who have the right stuff in them will rise to the top. And then — the crowning indignity — we readily look down on those who are unable to "rise" as being at the bottom of the social scale!

Margaret Mead asks, "If we demand that a man must succeed to be regarded as good, how difficult do we dare to make that success without running the risk of breaking the hearts and minds of the many who fail?"[9]

When a person's need goes unsatisfied for a long time, we say that he is *deprived*. If it is food he lacks, he satisfies that need by going to the refrigerator or a restaurant. But if the effort to reach his goal is thwarted, the result is frustration.[10] When Christians look to their church for the acceptance and love they need and don't find it, they are deprived. They experience frustration that is not only disappointing but personally damaging.

A woman met me in the hall as she came out of her Sunday morning adult Bible class. She admitted she didn't particularly enjoy the teacher. "I keep coming," she explained with un-expected candor, "because I need friends . . . but I'm not finding them."

It isn't enough to say to her, "Well, God loves you and that's all you need. Forget yourself and serve the Lord!" There is much more to be said *and done* in dealing with lovelessness among Christians.

This woman was not a "social climber," but she was reach-ing out to fulfil her need for satisfying relations with other Christians. Our psychologists tell us that the stronger the effort to reach a goal, and the nearer the goal seems to be, the greater the frustration that results if the goal isn't reached.

Finding satisfactory social relationships *anywhere* today — whether in sophisticated Suburbia, a big city, or a rural area — may be a problem, and perhaps disappointing. That is the kind of world we live in and the way human beings are.

But when we find our way into a group who are committed Christians in no merely nominal sense; when we understand something of the distinctives of Christianity, the teachings of Christ, and the professed belief of His followers in selfless love for one another, we are filled with great expectations. Here, certainly, we shall meet open hearts and faces, acceptance that is charitable, love that is warm and personal and practical. In this setting our "goal" seems almost within our grasp.

It is this enlarged hope that makes so terrible the frustration we feel when that so-near goal eludes us, when we are con-fronted with closed hearts, faces, and homes; with indifference if not disapproval and outright rejection.

It is high time for God's people to realize that many people experience such disappointment.

"Human adjustment can be said to be a perpetual battle against frustration. For some, the battle rages more savagely than for others. Some seem to be on the winning side, others seem to lose more often than they win."[11] And even those who don't feel rejected experience widely varying degrees of fulfillment in their church relationships.

Many survive out on the fringes somewhere, hardly ad-mitting to themselves, and certainly not to anyone else, that they are hungry for friends — for the kind of fellowship that would enable them openly to admit their real needs and find personal reinforcement from other Christians as well as from God. Still others eat their hearts out with longing to be included in some particular clique in which they aren't welcome (and perhaps wouldn't at all fit!).

Members of the congregation attend the same meetings and social functions week after week, greet each other politely, and even exchange some small talk, but sometimes, as one church-goer put it, "There are many meetings and little real fellowship."

"Our churches are filled with people who outwardly look contented and at peace but inwardly are crying out for someone to love them . . . just as they are — confused, frustrated, often frightened, guilty, and often unable to communicate even within their own families. But the other people in the church *look* so happy and contented that one seldom has the courage to admit his own deep needs before such a self-sufficient group as the average church meeting appears to be."[12]

A revealing discussion followed the asking of a disturbing question in a couples' group: "How many friends do you have on whom you could call for help in an emergency at two o'clock in the morning?" Many acquaintances, was the conclusion, but few friends in *that* category! Some people are satisfied with few close friends, or even prefer not to be involved in intimate relationships, but most would like to have at least a few close friends among their more numerous acquaintances. And almost anyone (not merely the left-outs) would like to have more friendships or more satisfying ones.

In *The Cocktail Party,* T. S. Eliot suggests that the reason the cocktail glass has become so important is that the Communion cup has lost its meaning. "The Communion cup," he explains, "represents a special relationship in which persons become close in fellowship and yet are most fully themselves. They find the mastery of Him who is their Lord."

Have you experienced that special relationship in which you are fully yourself but in which you become *close* in fellowship with other Christians under the complete control of your Lord?

3

WHY IT ISN'T LIKE IT WAS

What was so unusual about the first-century Christians' attitude toward other believers that provoked their contemporary, Tertullian, to say, "Behold how they love one another"? Jesus had prayed that His followers would be "one."[1] In spite of problems on the inside and threats from the outside, His prayer was conspicuously answered among those earliest Christians. Fellowship between them was quick and intimate. They met together, often daily, in the Temple or in homes. They greeted each other warmly "with a holy kiss," were concerned about each other's needs, shared their possessions, often cried when they separated, and traveled countless miles on foot to see and help each other.

How do you account for such affection?

A Person

First of all, these believers were bound together because each one had had a personal experience with a person — Jesus Christ. They had been confronted with the claims of this God-man who had appeared in their world, who had lived and died, risen from the dead, gone back to heaven, and promised to return. Even those who hadn't known Him personally were convinced by eyewitnesses who had examined

the evidence, decided to believe Jesus' claims, and — at terrible risk — became His followers. They turned themselves
over to Him and His plans because of what He was and what
He had done for them. He had healed their bodies, forgiven
their sins, and given them an answer to the riddle of life.
He was a Leader they could trust and worship.

Ready to stand with Him and for Him, they found themselves standing with each other, part of a lively minority, men
and women who also believed this Jesus of Nazareth was no
less than the Son of God and the Savior of sinners — themselves in particular.

Most early Christians were part of a relatively small group.
They were denounced by religious as well as political leaders,
often made fun of, excommunicated, jailed for their faith,
driven out of their homes and chased from city to city, or
sentenced to die. With such prospects, people didn't lightly
decide to become Christians. Only under strong conviction
and solid determination to follow Jesus at any cost would anyone publicly identify himself with this strange new group.

Unlike some religious professions today, this wasn't a step
anyone would take for personal advantage from the world's
viewpoint. Who, among the multitudes who ignored or rejected Jesus, would dare to leave the safe majority and take
his stand with the despised few — the followers of the Gali-
lean? Only those to whom this God-man had become more
important than anything else in the world!

What would be the attitude of other first-century Christians toward the brave new convert who stepped out to join
their small company? Can't you almost see the open arms and
hearts with which they received him — proud of him — proud
of the Lord who had brought them together, and realistically
aware of what it might cost to take such a stand?

Position and possessions should make little difference under
such circumstances. How could it matter whether a new convert was young or old, stylish or plain, rich or poor, prominent
or obscure? What really mattered was his relation to Jesus
Christ. That was ground enough for his acceptance into the
fellowship of other Christians.

Does social position, economic or professional standing, race or color make any difference *today* in the kind of reception a new Christian gets from other believers? Who would dare to say that it doesn't make a great difference in many churches — that one's personal experience of "Christian fellowship" isn't sometimes *determined* by such factors?

In many instances the reception of a new church member in this generation is no great occasion, and his personal relation to Jesus Christ not a matter of much concern. Some church rolls are loaded with the names of people who are only nominal Christians, poorly related to each other because actually they have never become personally related to God. No wonder the warm, shining personal relationships of first-century Christians are missing in many local churches today!

Have you ever noticed how widely assorted the guests at a bridal shower often are? Mothers, sisters, grandmothers or other relatives of the bride or groom; neighbors; young friends from school, the office, or church; older women who are friends of the couple's parents. This human assortment might not be socially compatible in any other situation, but here differences in age, material prosperity, or education are lost sight of in the light of their common relationship to the couple about to be married.

The guests, at least for the moment, are one because of their tie to the guest of honor, and they feel close to each other because their hearts and minds are centered on one thing — the person they all know and love.

This was the secret of oneness among the first Christians. A *Person* — Jesus Christ — had brought them together. John had this in mind when he wrote: "What we have seen and heard we tell you also, so that you will *join with us in the fellowship* we have with the Father and with his Son Jesus Christ."[2] Their personal differences were unimportant in the face of their enthusiasm for Him. Only when this enthusiasm cooled was the unique quality of the group corrupted by jealousy, the itch to dominate others, self-seeking, and snobbery.

A Group

Having fallen in love with a unique Person, the living Christ, these believers found themselves joined to a group known as Christians — the Church.

What was this group like?

First of all, it was distinct and conspicuous. The oneness of those who made up the early Church was an almost natural result of their being so necessarily separate from people all around them. The gulf between a Christian and the synagogue Jew or the Gentile idolator was enormous.

At first the Christians met in the Temple or synagogue, but later they had to gather in homes because they were excluded, hated, and persecuted by the Jews in their local communities.

The distinction between Christians and non-Christians was nothing uncertain or fuzzy. A Christian was a recognizable religious heretic, often viewed as an enemy of the state, and always as a radical and a freak. He was definitely "out," and in many localities was in danger of being arrested, put in jail, or killed. The individual Christian's feeling of closeness to other believers was intensified by his rejection and exclusion at the hands of neighbors, friends, and sometimes family.

Today it's easy (at least in the western world) to be classified as a Christian. Your life won't be in danger and you won't be put in jail. Your Christian profession may even involve no more than going to church a few times a year and maintaining a public image of respectability.

But that kind of "Christianity" doesn't produce the oneness among its adherents that New Testament Christians experienced. Today, instead of its being costly to become a Christian, one may take the step because it offers real social and business advantage. And it is usually impossible to distinguish Christians from unbelievers unless they wear the uniform of some sect or you see them sitting in a church pew. They may be well accepted in secular circles, and they are not discriminated against because they belong to a church. They may adopt a life pattern not visibly different from their neighbors' and feel as much a part of the world around them as of the local church to which they belong. They are not distinctively Christian — nor are they closely related to each other.

What did Jesus intend the relationship between His followers to be? As we look at the first-century Church we are, at this point, not so much concerned with its organization as with the personal relations inside it. What made possible the assimilation of such an assortment of individuals? And why isn't fellowship among Christians today always like that?

The New Testament Church broke out into history not just because men admired Jesus or were His friends, or because they went along with the new doctrines He taught. Their whole experience and message were centered in definite, well-documented historical facts and events — who Jesus was, what He had come to do, His words and His works, His death, and especially His miraculous physical resurrection. No mere set of teachings, no personal example could have produced such phenomenal results. Jesus' resurrection was the creative miracle. It was unique and spectacular, and the Christian Church was the result.

It was not only what *had* happened that bound Christians together, but also Jesus' promise that He would return. On the strength of what they knew about His recent coming to earth, these first-century Christians dared to believe His promise to come back again. It was a concrete, literal, exciting expectation. He would keep His word to them, and they would be ready for Him when He came.

A church feels the tingle of such expectancy when one of its own missionaries is scheduled to return after years of service in a faraway place. Neighbors share the thrill of an expected reunion when a family's son is about to come home after years of military service. And so the shared hope of Christ's return bound the early Christians together.

Christians today are nearly 2,000 years removed from that point in history when Christ came personally and visibly to our planet. The facts of His coming have never been discredited and are as historically reliable now as they were then. But many modern theologians, preachers, and teachers have lightly tossed them aside, labeled them "myths" and "symbols," or have at least given the impression that these facts have no important meaning for us. To multitudes of church-going men and women today the prospect of Christ's return to earth is unreal if not unheard of.

To those who still wear the label "Christian," but to whom the historical, alive-today Jesus has little significance, religion is primarily concerned with man's needs and problems, civic and political issues, and social service. Devotion to humanity, rather than to Jesus Christ, has become the mainspring of religious thinking and activity.

It is true that people also feel close to each other when they share a concern for human needs, but love for God and desire to please *Him,* in the long run, are the best guarantees that men won't lose their commitment to help each other. And love for God and His service is sparked at the fire of His love for us as shown at Calvary.

Assorted but United

These first-century Christians made up a colorful cross section of the human race. "God chose the poor people of this world . . . to possess the kingdom."[3] Paul wrote of the Christians in Corinth, "Few of you were wise, or powerful, or of high social status, from the human point of view. God . . . chose what the world looks down on and despises and thinks is nothing."[4]

But the upper crust were there too. In Jerusalem "the number of disciples grew . . . and *a great number* of the priests (prominent, influential leaders) accepted the faith."[5] In sophisticated and intellectual Greece, "many Greek women of high society and many Greek men also believed."[6]

And these assorted converts were different, too, in the gifts they exercised in the Church. Some could teach, some could pray, others were social workers, and some were officers in the group.

Christians came from different racial or national backgrounds, yet Paul dared to say, "There is no difference between Jews and Gentiles, between slaves and free men, between men and women: you are *all one* in union with Christ Jesus."[7] Of the then-despised Gentiles he declared, "You Gentiles are not foreigners or strangers any longer; you are *now* fellow citizens with God's people and members of the family of God!"[8]

There is a strong sense of oneness among people who have been saved from a common calamity — fire, flood, shipwreck, invasion, or imprisonment. The early Christians had each experienced deliverance from the ultimate disaster — God's fierce wrath against sin.

But merely nominal Christians, who have never admitted their own spiritual bankruptcy and cried to God for mercy, know little about the oneness that exists among those who have experienced His saving grace. And because they know little of His grace toward themselves in Christ, there may be little of that grace in their relationships with each other.

There was more than mere *union* among the assorted members of the first-century Church. There was *unity*. Someone has described the difference by saying that if you tie the legs of several chickens together and throw them over a clothesline you have union but not unity!

The early Christians were united not so much by outward organization as by the presence and supernatural working of the Holy Spirit in each of them — first in their own spiritual rebirth, and then His working in them to make them like Christ and through them to win others to faith in Him. This was God's own provision for the building of His church — different abilities, different gifts, different services to be performed, but by *one* Spirit and for *one* Lord. There was *one* body with many parts; one Shepherd with *many* sheep; *one* Father with a large family.

Jesus had said, *"I will build My Church,"* and these first believers were its beginning. He had guaranteed that the Church would survive and grow, and had sent the Holy Spirit at Pentecost to be its dynamic. Under that power the Church spoke its piece, and the record says, "Every day *the Lord* added to their group those who were being saved."[9]

This was not a man-made outfit. The very fire of God was in it and on it, not only to credential the infant church with impressive miracles, but — more importantly — to bring other men and women to personal faith in the Savior the Church proclaimed. There was oneness in the group because, whoever or wherever they might be, one Spirit was at work among them.

"True Christian fellowship — what the Greek New Testament calls *koinonia* — is the Spirit's gift to the Church. Yet this fellowship is critically lacking in the institutional church today. And this lack goes to the very heart of the impotence, rigidity, and so-called irrelevance of much of the modern church. . . .

"The Church today is suffering a fellowship crisis. It is simply not experiencing nor demonstrating that 'fellowship of the Holy Spirit' (2 Cor. 13:14) that marked the New Testament Church. In a world of big, impersonal institutions, the Church often presents itself to modern man as just another big, impersonal institution. The Church is highly organized at a time when its members are caring less about organization and more about community. One seldom finds within the institutionalized church today that winsome intimacy among people where masks are dropped, honesty prevails, and there is that sense of communication and community beyond the human — where there is actually the fellowship of and in the Holy Spirit."[10]

The early Church depended on the Spirit's supernatural power in the carrying on of God's business. But modern churches depend more largely on outstanding leaders, elaborate organizational programs, and highly developed promotional methods. Organization and methods have a legitimate place in the Church, but as someone has well said, when you depend on organization, you get what organization can do. And when you depend on the Holy Spirit, you get what God can do.

Many modern Christians have no understanding of the third Person of the Trinity, and little vision — let alone experience — of His supernatural working in their individual lives or in the operations of their churches.

All Christians Everywhere

The early Church not only made room for all kinds of unlike individuals but was geographically broad enough to include "all God's people scattered over the whole wide world."[11] There was a lively sense of belonging even between Christians who had never seen each other and never expected to see each other in this life. Wherever they were, they were bound together by the wonder and dignity of being part of the great body of believers in all parts of the world.

Jesus' strong sense of personal relationship to those who belonged to Him fills His prayer in John 17, which also makes it clear that He will never be satisfied until His followers have a keen sense of belonging to each other as well as to Him.

Endless divisions in the Christian Church have diluted the sense of oneness Christians once shared. They get bogged down by exclusive interest in their local church, or by denominational loyalties. But, says John Walvoord in discussing the current movement to unite all churches, "The hope of the Church today is not a world organization, but rather a realization of the unity *that already exists* in the body of Christ — that mystical tie which binds every believer to every other true believer."

The early Christians had to look at each other in the light of Christ's loving. He loved them all without discrimination — regardless of race, color, nationality, personal talents, or achievements. When the Ephesian Christians were in danger of losing sight of the broader reaches of Christian loving, Paul wrote, "I pray that you may have your roots and foundations in love, and that you, *together with all God's people,* may . . . understand how *broad* and *long* and *high* and *deep* is Christ's love."[12] If the perfect, sinless Son of God could love them in all their imperfection and unloveliness, how could they refuse to love each other?

Of everyone who believed in Christ, Paul said, "There is no difference at all"[13] because they had all sinned and needed to be put right with God through Christ. No matter who or what they were, they were all — as forgiven sinners — on one level before God, and received the same gracious acceptance. Jude wrote of "the salvation we share in common."[14]

No wonder Paul said that since all Christians stand on common ground, they have no right to brag or be snobbish.

And no wonder he added, "Accept one another, then . . . *as Christ has accepted you.*"[15]

To accept other Christians as Jesus does is a huge order. Acceptance means much more than tolerance. It means warm, persistent, shining love — in which there is no room for conceit, condescension, discrimination, or contempt. Such loving will be discussed in a later chapter, but it sets a pattern against which every sincere Christian must test his own attitudes.

It is hardly necessary to mention the discrimination that exists even in some (but not all) Christian circles. A black man is not allowed to enter the sanctuary of a church. Anyone who is not socially or economically acceptable is given the calculated freeze so that the quality of the group will not be lowered. Unattractive (or too attractive) teen-agers are made the butt of jokes and whisperings, are persistently and intentionally persecuted until they quit coming to the youth meetings. A woman who once had a bad reputation but has recently become a Christian finds no acceptance or friendship among the members of the church.

These attitudes have nothing in common with Jesus' acceptance of all who came to Him, His love for the undeserving and despised. That kind of love, when practiced among His followers, overcame personal prejudice and produced the rare fellowship in the early Church.

Changed Persons

But the quality of this unique group depended on much more than their merely accepting and loving each other. That was only part of the magic. These men and women were all involved in a process of being changed — of growing out of personal characteristics that were unlovely, irritating, selfish and corrupting, toward new actions and attitudes that belonged to the new life they were living.

This process of change was not automatic, but was made possible by the working of the Holy Spirit in each individual Christian. It involved more than having new goals or a new pattern for living. It was being set free from old ways and being made like Jesus Christ.

The change wasn't instantaneous or complete, as the New Testament frankly records. But the whole direction of these lives, as they let God work in them, was toward unselfishness, honesty, generosity, sexual cleanness, contentment, compassion, and love.

Such things as lying, jealousy, greed, and lust damage and destroy human relationships. So, for all the imperfections and shortcomings of these early believers, their relation to each other improved as each one experienced personal growth and renewal. Such personal improvement makes living in any society a better experience.

Is godliness — the building of Christian character — a major goal of Christian institutions today?

Churches ride all sorts of hobbies. Some are almost totally evangelistic — preoccupied with getting "sinners saved." Those who are already Christians get little food for personal growth, listen to endless presentations of God's plan of salvation, and sit through prolonged appeals to those present (often no unbelievers among them) to decide for Christ. They hear little about the changed life and Christlike character that should be the inevitable sequel to conversion.

Sometimes preachers are too good politicians to preach against wrong attitudes or particular sins that are common in their congregations. They talk about conditions in a disordered world, but are careful not to get too close to home. Their people know little about God's standards of rightness — the kind of character and personal relationships He approves in the home, the office, and the church.

Still other ministers are too preoccupied with defending sound doctrine, maintaining legalistic rules of conduct, or drawing denominational lines to be actively concerned about the spiritual maturing of their flock. Consistent Christian character doesn't develop — and Christian fellowship is no glowing affair.

In such settings unchristlike attitudes and actions flourish. Unchanged men and women react to each other much as they would if they had never encountered the living, life-transform-ing Christ. Fellowship in their company doesn't begin to resemble that of New Testament days.

Fellowship in the early Church also grew out of shared problems and a sense of responsibility to meet each other's needs. Christians shared their food, made clothing for the poor, arranged for care of widows, supplied financial help to poor Christians near and far, made provision for the needs of missionaries sent out to win new converts for Christ, and met together to pray and plan for expansion.

In many religious circles today, Christians know little about each other's personal needs and feel little responsibility when they do know. People sit side by side in a church pew once a week and never get acquainted with each other. When they do make a beginning, they put their masks firmly in place so that they will appear (like most other Christians) to have no personal problems or needs.

What happens when it *is* known that a fellow Christian is facing a crucial decision, temptation, criticism, illness, bereavement, rebellion in his children, unemployment, or foreclosure? Among some believers there is instant rally, loving concern, and practical helping. But sometimes *nothing* happens. The matter may get talked about, but few show concern or try to help. Actual sharing and meeting of personal needs would greatly reinforce the feeling of community between individuals in the Church.

New Testament Christians expressed their love for each other by practical help and kindness, but also in open, direct expressions of affection. The Apostle Paul repeatedly told his converts how much they meant to him, how he missed them and longed to know how things were going with them. He cared intensely about their needs — physical as well as spiritual — and, when he couldn't come to them, sent someone else to let them know he still loved them and was interested in them.

Even when he had occasion to scold his converts for misconduct, he told them plainly that he still loved them, and urged them to continue to express their love for each other with the brotherly kiss that was a common greeting in that culture.

Many Christians today who provide kind, practical help to each other hardly know how to tell another Christian that they thank God for him, love him, value his friendship, are concerned about his needs, and miss him when he's away. It's true that it isn't enough *just* to say it, but many a Christian would be encouraged by such simple expressions of affection.

The Individual Intact

The feeling of oneness among the early Christians didn't at all make the individual less important. The "Church" never ceased to be individual persons to its leaders. The New Testament is full of the names of people who were distinct in their minds and associated with particular situations.

Tabitha made shirts and coats. Barnabas was one of the first who dared to believe that the notorious Saul of Tarsus had actually been converted to Christianity. Rufus' mother is named because she treated the apostle "like a son." Of Phoebe, he wrote, "She . . . has been a good friend to many people, and also to me." Onesimus was a runaway slave who needed forgiveness from Philemon, his Christian master. Alexander was a rascally coppersmith, and Demas deserted Paul because he fell in love with worldly living.

Individual Christians didn't lose their personal identity or importance, and this was a strength rather than a weakness. But in many churches today the individual feels lost in the crowd. He attends worship services, study groups, meetings for men or women, denominational convenings, and — unless he holds a distinguished official position — comes away feeling that he isn't much more than a blur in the whole. If he stops attending, it is painfully clear that no one misses him.

Christian leaders, becoming aware of this situation, are looking for a new emphasis that is oriented more to the individual than to the group.

First-century Christians were also bound together by their shared interest and goal — telling others about Jesus Christ. They told about Him individually wherever they went, and sent and supported representatives who preached Christ in areas they couldn't personally contact. It's a well-known fact that people who are active in a common project enjoy a special relation to each other because of that shared activity.

What are the most urgent concerns for many churches today? Paying off the church debt? Enrolling new members to compensate for those who are losing interest? Maintaining elegance in the sanctuary, high caliber music, and denominational status? Financing (without personal participation) humanitarian projects in ghetto areas at home and mission fields abroad? Hiring an efficient pastor to do the soul-winning for the congregation?

Twentieth-century Christians, like the first-century variety, become one as they are individually and jointly active in winning others to Christ and bringing them into their fellowship for instruction and growth.

Disagreements and divisions between groups of Christians began to appear even in the New Testament era and are grotesquely multiplied today. However, for the purposes of this book, we are primarily concerned with relationships *within* a group of Christians rather than *between* groups.

Even in the first century, some Christians in a local church were more devoted to one leader and some to another. Paul wrote to the Corinthians, "When there is jealousy among you, and you quarrel with one another, doesn't this prove that you are . . . living by this world's standards? When one of you says, 'I am with Paul,' and another, 'I am with Apollos' — aren't you acting like worldly men?"[16]

Partiality and snobbery also had to be rebuked for class distinctions were being made at church meetings. "My brothers!" he wrote, "In your life as believers in our Lord Jesus Christ, the Lord of glory, you must never treat people in different ways because of their outward appearance.

"Suppose a rich man wearing a gold ring and fine clothes comes in to your meeting, and a poor man in ragged clothes also comes in. If you show more respect to the well-dressed man and say to him, 'Have this best seat here,' but say to the poor man, 'Stand, or sit down here on the floor by my seat,' then you are guilty of creating distinctions among yourselves.

"Listen, my dear brothers! God chose the poor of this world to be rich in faith and to possess the Kingdom which he

promised to those who love him. But you dishonor the poor!
. . . If you treat people according to their outward appearance,
you are guilty of sin."[17]

Notice that the rebuke here was not for failure to meet the
poor man's material need — to give him food or clothing —
but failure to accept his *person*, to treat him as the rich were
treated when the church came together. This incident was
told to plead the social need of the poorly-accepted church
member. So soon was the strength and beauty of Christian
oneness corrupted!

However, the glow and goodness of Christian fellowship
has not become extinct. Where Christians are simple enough
and wise enough, where Christ is central and His way of life
is put into practice, there is a kind of fellowship, of oneness,
that is unique, exciting, exhilarating, and satisfying. It isn't
always easy to find, but it's wonderful to experience!

4

LOOK AT YOURSELF — OTHERS DO

Barbara Stanley is an active but not too popular member of Community Church. She can — as she will readily declare — "see through" anyone on shortest acquaintance. She can tell you who talks too much, why the minister's sermon was below par last Sunday, the real reason why Jim Holman got elected to the Board of Elders, the basic character deficiency of the glamorous new co-ed in the youth group who "stole" her own daughter's boyfriend, and the unspirituality of Shirley Newman's new Easter outfit.

But Barbara Stanley is utterly unaware of her own faults and failings — blind as a bat to the unchristian motives and attitudes that underlie her confident analysis of other people.

If anyone wants to think realistically about his relationships with other Christians, he needs to look first of all at himself.

Everyone is familiar with his own exterior image — especially the face he views so often in the mirror. But did you ever ask such practical questions as: "What kind of person do people *think* I am? How do I carry myself — do I walk well? What do I talk about most? Am I friendly or snobbish?"

It may be easy to see why some people are well liked and others aren't so popular. But no one is going to walk up to us and do us the great favor of saying, "People would like you better if you took more baths," or "if you weren't such a whiner," or "if you didn't monopolize every conversation." Unfortunately, we usually have to discover these faults ourselves — and many of us never do.

It might be a good thing if adults had the desperate courage some young teens have. I have heard them ask and discuss, "What's wrong with me? Why don't some people like me?" And the answers were often specific and constructive. They have talked about why some of their peers were more popular. (Not all their reasons were complimentary!) The young people were practical and direct (not always merciful) in analyzing themselves and each other.

As you evaluate (that is, appreciate and criticize) the folks around you, remember that they in turn respond to you in certain ways because of the way you look to them. "O wad some power the giftie gie us to see oursels as ithers see us!"

Introspection can be overdone, but most Christians would profit by a little self-analysis and by getting a true view of themselves as they appear to others in their local church group. It could help them become personally more acceptable and condition them to meet the urgent needs of other Christians.

Look behind that well-placed mask you wear. Others do! If you are a well-accepted person, take a good look not at how great your special friends think you are, but how you appear to those who are *not* your particular intimates. If you are among the not-so-popular and feel ignored or rejected, ask why.

In later chapters we'll discuss the special needs of the *Ins* and the *Outs,* but for the moment, we're concerned with how Christians in general look to those around them.

This book deals with relationships within a group of *Christians,* whether they come together for worship, study, service, or fellowship.

A New You

People join Christian groups for a variety of reasons. Non-Christians should be warmly welcome, but to fit in as an organic part of the fellowship of God's people, one must himself be a Christian — personally related to God. This means coming into possession of *new* life through faith in Jesus Christ. If you haven't experienced this newness, it's foolish to try to reform your old self to fit God's specifications.

"So," Paul advised the Ephesian Christians, "get rid of your old self, which made you live as you used to. . . . Your hearts and minds must be made completely new. You must put on the new self, which is created in God's likeness."[1] On the basis of that newness, the apostle goes on to set standards about truthfulness, self-control, helping the poor, right talk, kindness, and forgiveness.

Be sure you *are* a Christian before you try to *act* like one! Have you, and others in your group, personally met Jesus Christ and committed yourselves to Him? Or are you a little like a butcher trying to fit into the International Brotherhood of Amalgamated Boiler Makers? A genuine conversion experience can quite transform your rapport with other Christians!

The new life God gives makes it possible for you to be delivered from the old self-life and to grow personally — especially in your capacity to love people. This is the very root of the goodness that should be found in relationships among Christians.

But before we think about other people's reactions to you, how do you feel about yourself? Even after you experience newness in Christ, many things about you will remain more or less the same.

Your nose will be the same shape, you'll be as short or tall, old or young, and have the same IQ as before. Your racial or cultural background will still be there; you will have the same parents and dispositional characteristics. For the time being, at least, you will have the same home, school, or business set-up.

You and God may change some of these things, but face up to what you are physically, mentally, and otherwise. Accept your face and figure (insofar as you can't improve them). If you are personable, thank God for it; if you are to some degree unattractive, face the facts about yourself, accept them, and then be your best possible self and enjoy being that.

It takes all kinds to make a world, and God is glorified when each of us accepts himself as he is without resentment or bitterness. When you have done that, you can begin to like yourself, and then other people will begin to like you in spite of your limitations.

Have you, as a Christian, ever been puzzled by the psychologists' stress on the importance of *loving yourself?* Does this seem to conflict with a Christian's goal of not being self-centered? Not at all! Jesus spoke of loving one's neighbor as oneself. We not only have a God-given instinct for bodily self-preservation but we owe it to ourselves to keep clean, healthy, and alert physically, mentally, and spiritually. Consciously or unconsciously, we don't like ourselves when we're dirty, lazy, or irresponsible, or when we're not people of moral and spiritual integrity.

F. A. Magoun, writing about the mainsprings of character, lists self-respect as one of the most important traits — "as important as life itself." He adds, "Robert Louis Stevenson said that a man . . . is above all to remain friends with himself. Obviously! He is the only person with whom he must live continuously, intimately, inescapably.

"Furthermore, every man stands trial in the courtroom of his own conscience and no man is ever acquitted. There is no appeal from himself no matter how desperately he tries to upset the verdict by rationalizing. Contrariwise, neither the ridicule nor the censure of other people can destroy the ability of a healthy self-respect to strengthen his life. . . . The opinions of other people are primarily other people's business. Honestly liking himself is very much a man's personal business, especially since it is not possible for him to remain friendly for long with someone he does not respect — particularly with himself."[2]

No Masks

You damage yourself and your relations with other people if you either underestimate or overestimate yourself. Take a modest, realistic view of yourself. Hugh Downs admitted to thinking he was intellectual until, on occasion, he found himself "a Chihuahua among St. Bernards." Learn to think of yourself according to what you know you are, not what others think you are. And don't wear a false front because you want to seem to be what you know you're not.

Author-professor Larry Richards says people wear masks because they doubt their own importance — they think they're not interesting enough, as they are, to be liked. Or they imagine themselves to be more than they are and have to prop up the image. Or they are afraid that people will find out that they're different from the crowd in some way — that they really like soap operas, detective stories, poetry, or classical music, or that they don't like baseball, pizza, opera, or praying aloud.

Actually, Richards advises, you're probably not as different as you think! And "no one can be confident when he's not what he seems to be. The strain gets worse; he gets lonelier and lonelier as he holds people off with his false front."[3]

A genuine conversion experience can quite transform your attitude toward yourself and set you free to be yourself — a changed and developing self — in relation to other Christians.

How does God set us free from our endless effort to impress people and win their liking? Paul Tournier reminds us that everyone has an "inexhaustible need to be loved and a continual fear of not being loved. . . . The truth is," he adds, "that God alone can fill the affective need of men; God alone is always there, in His limitless love."[4]

When you are sure that you have come into a personal relationship with God, you know, first of all, that you are accepted by Someone who sees you as you really are, who knows everything about you, yet doesn't reject you. More than that, you know that you are valued, that you are precious to Him. You can "throw the whole weight of your anxieties upon him, for you are his personal concern."[5] When this truth becomes real and important to you, your deepest need has been met and you can relate to people without being uneasy or desperate and without needing to pretend.

But even among Christians some get along with each other better than others. It's all very well to "be yourself," but be sure you are your *best possible* self. Some personal characteristics make folks enjoy you, others turn them off.

Take a quick trip through the following lists of positive and negative characteristics (all of them are subject to change) and rate yourself as realistically as your friends probably rate you. Some of these traits will be discussed more fully later.

Charles B. Roth reported an experimental psychologist's study of reasons why some people are liked and some disliked. The following list (parentheses added) of the ten most obnoxious personality traits is said to determine the fate of your personality "with almost matchless accuracy."[6]

1. Lack of dependability (Can people count on you?)
2. Grumpiness (Are you a chronic griper?)
3. Exaggeration (To make things look better — or worse!)
4. Tendency to show off (It helps the ego — or does it?)
5. Sarcasm (Are you noted for your ability to make it burn?)
6. Sense of inferiority (Does this cloud hang over you?)
7. Bossiness (Do people see you as overbearing?)
8. Tendency to criticize and find fault (Always, of course, in the interests of what is really right!)
9. Poking fun at people behind their backs (Great sport — but not for those you poke the fun at.)
10. Desire to dominate others (You may not even be aware of this hidden yearning.)

While you're at it, check yourself on a number of other traits that usually produce unfavorable reactions in the people who share your world:

Offensive talk. Do you talk too much? Is your voice loud or strident? Do you speak with a tone of finality that implies there is no more to be said on the subject? Or, are you a good listener, willing to give others "equal time" in a conversation?

Do you gossip? People may pay keen attention to the juicy tidbits you offer, but — knowing your wagging tongue — they will be slow to want you for a close friend. "Gossip is a dainty morsel eaten with great relish. . . . Fire goes out for lack of fuel, and tensions disappear when gossip stops."[7]

Superiority complex. Are you indifferent or snobbish toward people you consider beneath you or of no use to you? "There is one thing worse than a fool, and that is a man who is conceited."[8]

Phoniness. Do you try to be something you really aren't?

Elizabeth Strachan warned against becoming "just an accumulation of other people's characteristics or mannerisms, until you are never able to be yourself."

Irritability and *hypersensitivity.* Do people know you as "touchy" and quick to feel resentful, annoyed, or hurt?

Hot temper. "There is more hope for a fool than for a man of quick temper."[9]

Hard to work with. Do you have trouble keeping on good terms with co-workers on committees and projects?

Self-pity. Are you preoccupied with feeling sorry for yourself and your circumstances?

Self-centeredness. People who are all wrapped up in themselves are usually insensitive or uncaring about the needs of others.

Positively Nice

If you come up with a favorable score on these *negative* traits, you are giving people good reason not to hate you. But how do you rate on *positive* personal qualities that make people enjoy your company and that boost your chances for friendship and popularity?

Ask yourself whether you are —

Personally attractive? No matter how pretty or handsome you are or are not, do you always look your best? Are you clean? Neat? As well dressed as possible? "There is no reason why Christians have to look like the taillight of society when they are called to be the light of the world."[10]

Friendly, outgoing? Are you open to people or do you put up a protective hedge around yourself? Do you reach out to them or wait for them to reach out to you? Are you ready to accept others as they are, not just when they fit your specifications? Can you accept them even if you don't fully approve of things they do? Do you respect a person's right to disagree with you *even when you're sure you're right?*

Courteous and *gentle?* These attitudes will prevent hurt and friction in your church relationships. "Show a gentle attitude toward all."[11]

Patient? Are you patient with people's faults and failures?

With the peculiarities of elderly people? (You'll be old some-day, too!) With the exasperating ways of youth? (They're in the process of *becoming* God's men and women — give them time!) With the unattractive? (You might have been.) With the mean? (Christ died for them, too!) "Love is patient."[12]

Forgiving? Have you let God give you the grace to forgive those who have wronged you, even when they haven't asked for forgiveness? Or do you hold and nurse grudges?

Encouraging? Every person feels a need for encouragement and enjoys being with those who give it. "Use only helpful words, the kind that build up and provide what is needed, so that what you say will do good to those who hear you."[13]

Optimistic and *expectant?* Do you begin each day eagerly or view it as just another dull, unpromising round? Have you learned to forget the past and reach forward with anticipation for what God has for you in the future?

Responsive and *enthusiastic?* Some people are so mild they seem completely blah! They never enthuse about their own affairs or respond to the enthusiasms of others.

Kind and *tactful?* "Kindness makes a man attractive."[14] Complete frankness and bluntness are not necessarily virtues. If someone were to pay you ten cents for every kind word you have spoken, and collect five cents for every unkind word, would you be rich or poor?

Happy? Christians have every reason to be cheerful — even joyful. In a problem-conscious world, happy people are refreshing — and usually well liked.

Poised? Are you always in control of the situation, no matter what the complications may be? Do your resources in God make you feel adequate for whatever a day brings?

Generous? Do you like to give to others, even when there's no prospect of a return on your investment? Are you ready to give everyone the benefit of the doubt? Are you willing to give yourself to meet others' needs?

Slow to take offense? "A wise man restrains his anger and overlooks insults. This is to his credit."[15]

Years ago, a magazine article confronted me with two words that have become helpful personal goals for me: *simplicity* and *sincerity.* They challenge me to be simple and direct —

uncomplicated (never scheming or conniving) in my relations with other people; to say and do nothing for effect, to say only what I sincerely feel. It's good to be set free from pretense and tension in one's relationships.

Most of these personal assets are merely human qualities, but they are characteristics God means His people to have. He sent His Son into the world not simply to provide forgiveness for the sins we have committed, but to deliver us from all the unloveliness — the ugliness — that sin produces in the relations of human beings to each other.

And He does more than merely hold up a model of what He wants us to be. He makes it possible for every Christian to become that kind of person. What isn't possible with men *is* possible with God. *Supernatural* power is put at your disposal for this exciting personal development. And when you become the person God means you to be, you will not only be pleasing to Him but more attractive to people.

The director of a coffee house designed to win young people to Christ discussed the qualifications for becoming a team member. "People are not *persuaded*," he told his candidates. "They're *attracted*. We must be able to communicate far more by *what we are* than by what we say."

Many Christians are well acquainted with the first verses of Romans 12, but sometimes they get so preoccupied with the negative — "Do not conform outwardly to the standards of this world," that they never get on with the positive business that follows: "Let God *transform* you inwardly by a complete change of your mind." To some degree we can change our outward conduct, but only God can make that radical change on the inside that will transform all we are and do.

Do you need to be different? Are your relationships with other Christians and your usefulness to Christ limited by things in you that need to be changed? God is able to change you if you will depend on Him to do it.

It's good to look at yourself honestly and ask, "How do others see me?" But for healthy self-examination take the advice of a great Christian, the late Kenneth Strachan of the Latin America Mission: "Never think of yourself *apart from God.*" Be careful to keep God in the picture whether you view your shortcomings or your good qualities, your failures or your successes. This will deliver you from discouragement and depression, and from self-satisfaction and smugness.

"Search me, O God, and know my heart; test my thoughts. Point out anything you find in me that makes you sad, and lead me along the path of everlasting life."[16]

5

LOOK AT OTHERS

How do you feel about people — about all the human beings who inhabit your particular world?

Are you interested in people in general or are you for the most part indifferent? Do you reach out eagerly to them wherever you find them, or protectively pull your skirts about you and let them go their way?

Would you rather be alone than with people?

Do you find getting to know people usually rewarding? Or disappointing?

Do you love all the Christians you know?

Are you warmly friendly to *everyone* in your church group?

Do you have some friends you enjoy and see more often than others? Is that cliquishness?

Do you think cliques are wrong?

Are you open to ideas that might improve your personal relationships with other Christians?

You and People

How you feel about people is important for three reasons, among others: First, it affects (if not determines) the way they feel about you. Second, it has a lot to do with how much you enjoy life. Third, it shows clearly your attitude toward God.

Perhaps you are one of those Christians who are attractive, warm, happy, friendly, outgoing persons. You enjoy people and people enjoy you. You have no social problems because you have good rapport with the human race. You may, by nature or environment, be socially well-adjusted. Or this ability to make touch with people may be the result of your personal relation to Jesus Christ. You have been delivered from self, set free from its over-sensitivities and demands for attention, and refocused so that your first interest is reaching out and ministering to others for Christ's sake. For you this is not so much a duty as a delight.

If a church has even a small minority of such members, they can be a tremendous addition to the local fellowship of Christians.

Perhaps you have decided that you don't need people, that your life is full enough with your family and other responsibilities. Or maybe people have disappointed you. When you trusted them, they let you down. Or perhaps you pretend you don't need friends because you've been rejected in the past and don't want to risk that failure again.

Lepp believes that people who claim to prefer to be alone usually unconsciously resent others' not accepting them.

It's true that while some people are naturally more outgoing and gregarious, others are constitutionally content to be alone.

But there's a difference between solitude and isolation. Everyone needs to know how to be alone some of the time and enjoy it. "To love solitude and to hate isolation" is the slogan of the brotherhood of Christian intellectuals in Cluny. There's nothing unhealthy about liking to be alone at times, but one is sick who prefers isolation — complete separation from people.

Even though some rugged Christians may profess no interest in being personally accepted by others, this doesn't at all clear them of responsibility toward the many who need and long for acceptance and friends.

It's certainly true that when you wall yourself off from people — keep them at arm's length and act as though you don't need or want any closer relationship — they sense it. The message gets through, whether it registers consciously or unconsciously. Folks learn that people are just not your dish.

You can do without them, and presto — they can do without you.

Strangely enough, you may cloak this attitude in a robe of super-piety: God has accepted you and loves you, and, that's quite enough for you! Actually, such an attitude makes you appear snobbish — closed to people — and shuts you off from opportunities to know and help meet personal needs around you.

The truly "spiritual" Christian will be open, available, reaching out to touch others. People instinctively sense this availability and respond to it.

An attitude of relaxed openness to people can come to you if you really want it. It happened to me. I had friends and enjoyed people, but I was a person of high sensitivity and some social insecurity. I was too much aware of people's reactions.

But God has been teaching me to be more interested in others than in their reactions to me. He is setting me free from myself in my contacts with people — free simply to be interested in *them* and to open myself to whatever the relationship may offer.

Much later in life than we should have, my husband and I have decided that the most wonderful thing in the world — besides God — is people. All kinds of people! There is more adventure in human relationships than in any amount of sightseeing and travel. And this adventure is available to everyone.

After years of working with adults in our church, we branched out (after passing the fifty milestone) to working with college-age young people. We were scared to death at the prospect, but thoroughly enchanted with the experience.

Now we have moved to a retirement community (though we ourselves are not retired) and we still find the human race fascinating. Older people are interesting too, and rich in experience. Each one is a person in his own right — like or unlike ourselves — intriguing and rewarding.

Like us, each one has his imperfections, and some things about him may be offensive. But back of any unloveliness is a person — a human being like ourselves, loved of God, one for whom Christ died. And if this person is a believer he is in a special way our brother in Christ. We are members of the same family!

When you look at other Christians — any of them — remember this: Whether you like or dislike them, you belong to them and they belong to you! You can't decide whether you will be related to them or not. You *are already related* in a vital, supernatural, never-to-end way. "We're not separate units but intimately related to each other in Christ."[1] We are all members of the body of Christ — a mysterious, dynamic togetherness.

Paul described it this way: "Christ is like a single body, even though it is made up of different parts. . . . The body itself is not made up of only one part, but of many parts. . . . God put every different part in the body just as he wished . . . so there is no division in the body, but all its different parts have the same concern for one another. If one part of the body suffers, all the other parts suffer with it; if one part is praised, all the other parts share its happiness. . . . All of you, then, are Christ's body, and each one is a part of it."[2]

There may be some people in your local church group who are not actually members of that body because they have never come into a personal relationship with Jesus Christ. But if your church is the right kind of church, most of those who belong to it belong to Him, and your relation to them is a permanent one. So learn to live with them and love them now as well as forever!

How much you enjoy life will depend to a large degree on how much you enjoy the human race — people in general, not just a chosen circle of special friends.

The Sure Index

More important than your own pleasure — your attitude toward people is a sure index to your real attitude toward God. If you're a Christian, you can't afford to overlook your personal score in this area.

God loved the world and everyone in it so much that He gave His Son to meet their need.[3] While men were still sinners, unattractive and even repulsive to a Holy God, Christ came to be their Savior. Included as you were in that great goodness, you responded to His love, experienced His salvation, and now — with God's new life in you — you share the outgoing of His big heart to all men. (Or do you?) All men — and especially Christians — are included in His loving and in yours. (Or are they?)

Since God loved us when we didn't deserve it, we are left with no excuse if we refuse to love people who don't quite suit us. And more than that, God has *commanded* us to love one another.

Are you obedient to that command? Or do you reserve the right to measure and judge your fellow Christians? We sometimes forget that that is God's business. Our business is to measure ourselves by His standards and to love His people with the same patience He has shown in His attitude toward us.

Take a good look at the people who make up your world — especially those in your local group of Christians. Look at them as though you had never seen them before — those teenagers who whisper in church; the tactless usher who told them to shut up or get out; that stylishly dressed woman who is finding it hard to handle both her love for Christ and the social obligations her husband's position demands of her; that drab-looking woman who hasn't any style at all; the very short man who compensates for his size by being domineering; your pastor's wife, who is embarrassed by the rebellion of her teenage son. Try to see them as God sees them. His heart is open to them all, but He is counting on you to accept them and *show* them that you love them *as they are* and for His sake.

A young man explaining how he came into a personal relation to Christ said that for a long time he had been unable to accept the fact of God's loving him as he was. Then he married, and — for the first time in his life — was exposed to another person's intimate, increasingly complete knowledge of him. To his relief, his wife kept on loving him in spite of all she learned about his weaknesses and failures. This acceptance and love at last made it possible for him to believe that God loved and accepted him, and a real sense of relationship to God followed. Does your love make God's love believable to those who feel unworthy?

God sees the shortcomings and differences in people more clearly than you see them. Some of His children are grown up — spiritually mature; others are childish. Some are capable of leadership; others are not. Some are black; others are white. Some are too rigid and legalistic; others are careless and worldly. But He still loves them all and makes Himself available to them. Someone has well said, "God's love sets no limits and builds no fences."

Personal relationships in many churches would be transformed if Christians accepted people as Jesus did. He chose Matthew, a despised tax gatherer, and immortalized a poor widow whose contributions to the Temple budget were embarrassingly small. He made Himself available to children as well as to adults, and was not too holy to reach out to disreputable sinners.

I Love All of Them?

Even the most committed Christian sometimes faces a seeming impasse when confronted with the prospect of "loving" certain individuals. We ask, "How can we *love* people we don't *like?*"

We forget that Christian love — God's kind of loving — is not primarily a matter of feeling. When God loved fallen man He didn't "like" him in the sense that He approved or admired him. God hates sin, but He chose to love sinners. It was a decision, an act of the will. God acted in love toward those who didn't deserve it. He "set" His love upon them, made plans for their redemption, opening the way for them to come into a personal relationship with Himself.

There are unlovely people in the world and in the Church. God doesn't ask you to pretend that they are perfect or even likable. But He does ask you to do what He has done — love them as they are. This calls for an act of the will on your part, a decision to see beyond an individual's faults to the person himself — a human being of infinite value (who knows why?) to God — and to love him for Christ's sake.

If you don't *feel* loving toward this unattractive or disap-

pointing person, you can still *act* in love toward him. You are
not being a hypocrite as you try to understand his needs and
do what you can to meet them. You are being obedient to
God, who has commanded His children to love each other.

> He tames the savage beast
> In our behavior
> And binds us to Himself,
> Our Lord and Savior.
>
> Nor to Himself alone
> But to each other —
> "If you love me," He said,
> "Love one another."
> — S.E.W.[4]

The motive for such loving is your love for Christ. Jesus
said, "If you love me, you will obey my commandments."[5] . . .
"This is my commandment: love one another, just as I love
you."[6] John adds, "If someone says, 'I love God,' yet hates
his brother, he is a liar. . . . He who loves God must love
his brother also."[7] And the beautiful part is that usually,
when we act lovingly, loving feelings will follow.

When I find it hard to love someone I dislike or resent,
the best remedy for me is simply to remember the many things
in spite of which God has mercifully loved me. (Our smallest
sins are more repulsive to a holy God than the grossest sins
are to us.) Then — since God loves me — I can surely love
the other person in spite of anything.

But God has given more than a command and high motives
for loving each other. He has given supernatural power to do
it — to do what we could not do of ourselves. The "new birth"
you experienced when you put your trust in Christ put a new
kind of life in you — God's life. If you let Him, He will love
people through you, and you will discover what Paul prayed
the early Christians would come to know — "how broad and
long and high and deep is Christ's love."[8]

We sometimes balk at starting to love certain people, but
that is only the first step. We are to *"keep on* loving one
another as brothers in Christ."[9] In spite of obstacles, in-
justices, and disappointments, our love is to continue. "Love

never gives up."[10]

Years ago my husband and I decided that no matter what happened between us and the relatives in our families — what they did or didn't do — we would just forget anything that seemed hard to take and act as though nothing had happened. It has proved to be a delightful arrangement for getting along with relatives. And it can be just as delightful in relationships with other Christians.

Getting along with people is costly. It cost God *everything* to show His love for us, and living in love with those who make up our Christian community may require setting aside our own self-importance, our convenience, and even our rights. But the dividends are great!

How will Jeff act when Howie, a newcomer, beats him in the election of a president for the youth group? Or how will Jeff's mother react when she isn't invited to a shower given by a member of her Sunday school class? Will they keep on loving?

Loving others for Christ's sake will first of all put an end to much of the scathing criticism the world hurls at the Church because of friction among its members. "This is God's will: he wants you to silence the ignorant talk of foolish men by the good things you do. . . . Respect all men, *love your fellow believers.*"[11]

Secondly, living in love with other Christians is not only impressive evidence to the critical world that looks in upon us, but also reassures the individual Christian that he actually does have a personal relation to God. "Let us love one another, for love comes from God . . . if we love one another, God lives in us and his love is made perfect within us."[12] "We know that we have left death and come over into life . . . because we love our brothers."[13]

Christians who can't get along with other Christians had better consider God's startling statement: "Whoever does not love does not know God, because God is love."[14] If we react to people in the same way we would if we were not Christians, we'd better examine our personal relation to Jesus Christ.

And it is not enough simply to say you love other Christians, nor even to feel loving. Love is a lively, active thing that will *show* itself. "This is how God *showed his love* for us: he sent his only Son into the world that we might have life through him."[15] How do you show your love for the Christians around you?

Love is Friendly

Be habitually friendly to everyone.

My neighbor's young daughter dreaded entering the sixth grade because she was new in town and knew no one in her school. But much to her and her parents' amazement, a few weeks later she was elected president of her class. When asked how this happened, she said simply, "I guess it's just because I decided to be friendly to everyone in the class."

When Jesus told His disciples that they were to be "perfect" (that is, mature) people, He said, "You have heard . . . 'Love your friends, hate your enemies.' But now I tell you: love your enemies, and pray for those who mistreat you, so that you will become the sons of your Father in heaven. For he makes his sun to shine on bad and good people alike. . . . If you love only the people who love you . . . if you speak only to your friends, have you done anything out of the ordinary? Even the pagans do that!"[16]

God's plan for personal relationships among His people goes far beyond this! Each one is to be open, friendly, loving, self-giving to everyone. Paul felt "an obligation to all peoples, to the civilized and to the savage, to the educated and to the ignorant."[17] We are to offer open acceptance to *every* individual we meet — as one black Christian put it, "eyeball to eyeball." That is, with no air of being above or below another in our offer of friendship.

"Genuine Christian love is expansive, not exclusive, open, not selfish. It builds others up. It does not simply satisfy our ego and our need for security."[18]

There is real adventure in being friendly to all sorts of people. "A lively and friendly curiosity about people around us who lead lives that are quite different from ours can add spice and enrichment to our own . . . even if there is no particular desire to develop personal friendships."[19]

Hortense Calisher, discussing the lost art of friendship, says that we mistake the mannerisms of friendship for the emotions of friendship. We like to think we're "friendly" when we shake hands and smile. But we offer genuine acceptance and friendship only to our buddies.[20] This is an area of failure many Christians have never considered nor admitted.

Knowing the subject of this book, a friend who had moved twice since last we attended the same church wrote me some of her personal feelings about friendliness among Christians. She and her husband are distinguished people in the business world and equally distinguished as committed Christians, greatly used by God.

This is part of her contribution to the subject: "It is interesting to me to note — and this has been consistent — that the more liberal the church, the more friendly and concerned the people were. It was especially true in C____. We first attended a liberal church there, and folks were *so* nice, even offering to help find us an apartment. The church office called twice to see if they could help us in any way.

"In a more evangelical church we also attended, we were largely ignored. I've noticed that in the more evangelical churches they nearly knock you down in the aisle to get out to talk to their special friends." Then she added, "I make it a practice to look around and find someone who is standing alone and go over and talk with him."

These general observations wouldn't always hold true, of course, but they deserve consideration. Even though unfriendly churches may be found in either the liberal or the conservative camp, they certainly ought not to be found among those who insist that the Bible is the very Word of God and that one's attitudes towards people are to be determined by it.

The following article, "Was This Your Church?", appeared in *Power for Living*:

"I was a stranger in the city. The church sign read, 'Welcome,' so I went in. I smiled at the Sunday school children as they rushed to their classes. Neither they nor their parents greeted me. After I sat down, an elderly woman sat beside me. We exchanged names and shook hands. Another woman joined us, saying it was nice weather. After singing a few songs, we went to class. No one spoke to me.

"After Sunday school everyone rushed to the worship service. The service included hearty singing, prayer, and a beautiful duet. The minister welcomed Mr. and Mrs. So-and-so. 'I don't see anyone else I don't know,' he said, and then went on with announcements. After the closing prayer, I waited expectantly to meet someone, but over 100 worshipers filed out, not even pausing to say, 'It was good that you came today.'

"Big words in the bulletin said, 'Welcome, we are glad you came. Come often.' But all I could think was, 'I was a stranger and ye took me not in.' "[21]

Have you had similar experiences away from home, visiting in a strange church?

One winter my husband and I spent several months visiting adult Sunday school classes in our metropolitan area. We were appalled at the indifference of so many Christians toward strangers in their midst. In a usually small adult class we would perhaps be introduced as visitors, but often *no one* in the class — including the teacher — talked to us, showed any personal interest, or invited us to come again.

Most strangers don't want to be made a great deal of when they visit, but they may be looking for friends, for a church home, for spiritual help — so don't let them down. Greet them warmly, show a personal interest in them, and introduce them to your pastor or some member of the congregation near you.

Carefully remember their names and use them when you see them again. I often jot down the names of strangers, along with some clue to their appearance — "hook nose," "no chin," or "looks like a hamster" — and then pray that I won't lose the list for someone to find!

If you're not sure whether a person is a stranger or not, you can meet him with some safe remark such as "I probably should know your name but . . ." If he has been there before, he will supply the name, and if he is a first-timer he'll introduce himself.

Sometimes I simply say casually, "I'm Mrs. Jacobsen," and they respond with their names. No matter how unsure you may feel about approaching a stranger, do it with warmth and a smile — and a sense of adventure. Who knows what this contact may lead to?

Know People

Being friendly involves getting to *know* people. That casual "How are you?" greeting as you leave the church won't do it. You *can* ask "How are you?" in a way that lets folks know you *mean* it (if you do!). Be interested enough to want to know more about the other fellow.

Show an interest in his job and his family. It won't be easy to know which are his children, since the younger members are often in Children's Church and many teens don't sit with their parents, but nothing will more quickly build the bridge of friendship with a family than taking an interest in the children.

There is an urgent need for Christian young folks to feel accepted by the adults in their church, as well as by their own family and peers. Too often Christian adults view the young people in the church only with criticism, distaste, or indifference. And too often Christian young people look at older Christians with disrespect if not contempt.

Our college-age daughter, visiting our new church home for the first time, was impressed with the friendliness of the adults in the church as well as of those her own age. She was quite overwhelmed by their warm welcome and interest in her — especially by the charming couple who actually invited her to their home for a weekend.

Are you friendly to the young people in *your* church?

Young people, are you friendly to the adults and older people in your church? They will like you and enjoy you *if you give them a chance!*

Anyone has some good qualities and interesting experiences to share if you get to know him. Sometimes people will surprise you. King Solomon discovered that "some rich people are poor, and some poor people have great wealth!"[22] But you'll never discover the richness of the person behind that carefully arranged exterior unless you make the effort to know the individual. Don't make up your mind about a person until you do.

Put the best possible construction on his actions, and always give him the benefit of the doubt. If you're habitually critical of people in your mind — if you silently analyze their shortcomings, and try to conceal feelings of jealousy or contempt — they will unconsciously sense this and brush you off because in your mind you have already brushed them off. But just as surely, people will sense it when you meet them with warm, friendly feelings and genuine interest.

When you step into a room full of people, what are you thinking about? Are you focusing on yourself — how you look, how people will react to you, whether or not they will be friendly and talk to you? Or do you focus on the pleasure of being with these folks, anticipating the contacts, eager to enjoy them, to get better acquainted, to become aware of personal needs, to give yourself in any possible way to them?

Such an attitude is absolutely essential if you are to get along well with people. If your attitude needs changing, with God's help you can change it. And it can transform your personal relationships with people. I know because *I* needed changing.

Too Risky

As we have said, many people have stopped trying to be friendly because at some time they experienced rejection. Someone didn't respond to their move of friendliness, and because they were hurt they aren't about to risk rejection again. So they make a point of keeping a measure of coolness in their "friendliness," so no one will think that they are reaching out for friendship or that they need acceptance.

Take the risk! Show that you feel friendly. Expose yourself to the possibility of rejection; become vulnerable to people. You'll gain more than you'll ever lose. Most people are friendly and respond to friendliness. If sometimes your offer of friendship isn't reciprocated, you're no less a person than if you hadn't tried.

Even Jesus experienced rejection. And the Apostle Paul wasn't always loved in return. He wrote to the Corinthians,

"We have opened wide our hearts . . . it is you who have closed your hearts to us. . . . Show us the same feelings that we have for you. Open wide your hearts."[23]

If you take the risks of friendliness for Christ's sake, you don't have to feel embarrassed or ashamed when others don't respond. You have pleased Him, even if you haven't pleased someone else. And you will be more than compensated when the risk of friendliness pays off, as it often does, in unexpected directions. Perhaps someone feels left out, or discouraged, and hopes someone will say, "Good morning," or a person is new and eager to get acquainted, and your reaching out meets that need.

I once asked a prominent young lawyer in the church where I was assistant to the pastor, to call with his wife on a new young couple living in an apartment near them. They agreed with a little reluctance, but literally glowed when they reported on the visit. The new couple were not only eager for friends, but played stringed instruments, as did their visitors, and this dutiful first contact developed into a long-lived friendship.

I shall never forget the personal testimony of a young college professor who had been impressed by Christ's position on the cross — His arms outstretched so that they could be of no use to protect Himself, and His person completely exposed and vulnerable. Rather than defend Himself, Jesus, of His own free will, offered Himself to be the Savior and Friend of sinners.

"It was there at the cross," this young man told us, "that I learned the importance of not protecting or defending myself, of being willing to be open, to expose myself to people, making myself available to their need without being afraid of the risks involved."

This young man was excited at the new freedom he had discovered in his human relationships — freedom from the need to protect himself from hurt or humiliation, freedom from the tensions and restrictions he had once known in his contacts with students, friends, and strangers.

That freedom is available to you when you are willing to forget yourself and be consistently friendly to everyone.

The fellowship of Christians would be transformed if every

believer presented an open heart and face to every other member of his group. As I think about Christians I have known over the years, some stand out because, whether or not they were my close friends, I instinctively knew that they were open to me — available. Their Christian loving extended to me right where we were when we met. That is a good feeling and can be experienced even where there is no closely formed personal friendship.

Cliques?

What about "closely formed personal friendships"? If Christians are to love everyone and not discriminate, does that make it wrong for them to have special friends — people they want to spend more time with than they do with some others? If they have a group of friends they especially enjoy, does that condemn them as "cliquish"?

"God treats everyone alike."[24] He doesn't discriminate against certain individuals or groups. After Peter learned a hard lesson, he wrote, "I now realize that it is true that God treats all men alike."[25]

But God *does* select some people for special purposes. He chose the seed of Abraham, Jacob and not Esau, Saul and not his brothers.

Jesus "called to Himself the men He wanted" to become His disciples. To these twelve selected followers Jesus said, "I have chosen you to stay with me."[26] They were to be His close friends as well as preachers of His message.

Jesus spoke to the multitudes in parables, "but when he was alone with His disciples he would explain everything to them."[27] Jesus made Himself available to everyone — rich or poor — but He revealed Himself in a special way to a limited group. Mary, Martha, and Lazarus of Bethany were among these close friends to whom He turned when the pressures of life were great.[28]

God's people today, too, need friends as well as acquaintances. Ignace Lepp says, "My long practice as a depth psychologist has enabled me to verify the important role friendship can play in promoting authentic existence and to observe the distress of those who are deprived of it."[29]

We have the right to choose friends, to enjoy being part of a certain group of friends. We select one person as a life partner, others for specialized advice, for recreational activities, for employees, for good conversation and sharing experiences. Even Jesus had a closer relation to John, James, and Peter than to the rest of His disciples.

A young woman who was not finding the reality she longed for in her relationship with God increased the length of her personal devotions and attended more of the regularly scheduled meetings of her church, including the prayer meeting in the middle of the week. When she continued to feel this pressing lack, she shared her need with her pastor.

He advised her to get a prayer partner who would join with her in sharing what they found in their Bible reading and personal experience with God. This completely transformed her own experience — and another's — of the reality of Jesus Christ in one's life.

It's good to have close friends, but when a friend is also a Christian you have infinitely more in common, a more solid basis for friendship that is rich and lasting. But many Christian friends never dip into that reservoir of richer relationship because they won't honestly admit their real needs nor talk about the wonderful Lord they have in common.

Perhaps the best beginning in this direction is simply to admit a real need and ask your friend to pray about it. And when the prayer is answered, or other good things come into your life, share the good news with this friend and relate it to the One who is the Giver of every good gift.[30] This is no pretense at being pious, but is sincerely sharing what God means in your everyday life.

But we can't possibly include as *close* friends everyone we know. There just isn't enough time, nor enough of us, to form intimate friendships with many individuals.

Only with a few can we become free to share our most personal needs and problems. Openness just isn't easy until we know a person well enough to trust him, to hope that he will still accept and love us when he discovers our weaknesses and failures. But as you commit yourself to a person in this way, you also make it possible for him to be himself with you without pretending or being afraid.

Many Christians lack such friendships. They would like to have them, but the developing of this kind of relationship takes time and effort. It isn't enough to "entertain" a friend, or return an invitation, once or twice a year. It involves making casual contacts more often — thoughtful, practical caring, and willingness to take the risk of offering friendship.

This popular song shows how today's youth feel about the need for friendliness:

> This world's a lonely place to walk around in,
> this world's a place where life is hard to spend,
> but we can help each other live;
> everyone can give
> the simple gift,
> the words that lift —
> be my friend.

> Some days you wake up feeling nothing but fear,
> some days you wonder why God put you here;
> then all at once there comes a word —
> what was that you heard?
> Why, someone said
> from Gilead —
> be my friend.

> This life may not bring much of comfort to you,
> this world may lose its touch of kindness too,
> and who's to blame?
> Why can't you see?
> Only you and me . . .
> so if I may
> I'd like to say
> be my friend.*

Lepp says that a person may lack friends because he is too busy, too loaded with responsibilities to "welcome" another. He lacks time or "the emotional energy necessary for friendship." Or he may be "unavailable for inward reasons" — not really interested in others, self-centered. He "would like to

---

have a friend, but only for the egotistical satisfaction the other might provide."

It is flattering to have friends, to have people prefer your company and pay attention to your needs. But unless you are rich or famous, this isn't likely to happen without your making a sizable investment of yourself and your time in friendship.

You need at least a few close friends. If you lack them, ask God to direct you not only to those who will meet *your* need, but to those who also may need loyal, loving friendship. The Lord knows how to work such things out if you're willing to trust Him, to make yourself available to others, and to wait patiently while He acts.

And when we find someone with whom we share common tastes (a fondness for Bach or Pat Boone, Agatha Christie or T. S. Eliot) or common interests (baseball, knitting, or gardening), or common problems (teen-agers, mothers-in-law, asthma), we don't displease God, nor should it offend other Christians, that we specially enjoy these friends.

Cliques are wrong when members of a select group simply turn inward to each other and ignore or snobbishly exclude outsiders from their personal interest and love.

Enjoy an evening with your special friends, go to a football game together on Saturday if you will, *but* when Sunday rolls around don't get into a huddle with this bunch at the close of a church service. Don't *always* sit with them at church social events. If anything, see less of them there, and major in enjoying and reaching out to other members of your church family. Take an interest in *their* personal needs and in important events in *their* family circles, and share something of your own life situation with *them.*

Young and Cliquish

One of the major problems of youth work in the church is the cliquishness and snobbery that are so often characteristic of young people. Maryanna Johnson, writing about why social events planned for church young people often flop, recognizes this tendency to divide into cliques. Genuine group fellowship, she observes, is hard to achieve when newcomers are

left to themselves instead of being welcomed and included,
when young people are aloof in classes, bored in the adult
worship services, and lonely at their own socials.[31] These
obstacles sometimes seem insurmountable, and many a young
person has left the church because of this cliquishness.

One high-schooler told how the *In* group of young people in
her church "hated" the public school "socialites" — a strata
of students who were distinguished as not being "grease," were
socially popular, and maintained a quite rigid degree of exclusiveness. The critical church kids, said their peer, looked
with contempt (and spiritual superiority!) upon this group as
"snobbish," and liked to think that they themselves were not
admitted into it only because they were Christians.

Actually, this particular church bunch would probably never
have been admitted even if they hadn't been Christians. And
the quality of their Christianity stood in doubt because these
holier-than-thou young people reproduced in their own church
world the same snobbish exclusiveness they condemned in the
"socialites." They arbitrarily determined who was to belong to
their *In* group, and made a business of excluding, ignoring, or
showing contempt for other young people in the church.

How easy it is for those who have been excluded to fall
before the temptation to enjoy excluding others — to relieve
their own feeling of inferiority by acting superior to someone
else! This sort of cliquishness is completely out of order among
Christians — young or old. God hates it. Excluded Christians
bleed under it, and snobbish Christians will have to answer to
God for it.

Read the book of Proverbs, preferably in a modern translation such as *The Living Bible* (the edition for young people
is called *Get Smart*).[32] It is a practical, down-to-earth man-
ual on friendship.

"A mirror reflects a man's face, but what he is really like
is shown by the kind of friends he chooses."[33]

"Some people are friends in name only. Others are closer
than brothers."[34]

"Love forgets mistakes; nagging about them parts the best
of friends."[35]

"It is harder to win back the friendship of an offended

brother than to capture a fortified city. His anger shuts you out like bars."[36]

"If you shout a pleasant greeting to a friend too early in the morning, he will count it as a curse."[37] (Contemporary application: early telephone calls!)

"Don't visit your neighbor too often, or you will outwear your welcome!"[38]

"Never abandon a friend — either yours or your father's. Then you won't need to go to a distant relative for help in your time of need."[39]

"Wounds from a friend are better than kisses from an enemy."[40] (Avoid hurting a friend, and forget it if he offends you.)

"Good news from far away is like cold water to the thirsty."[41] (Keep in touch with friends who are away.)

Imperfect as some Christian loving may be, the Church of Jesus Christ *should* be — and often is — your best bet if you're looking for personal acceptance and practical love. And where Christian fellowship does fall short of what God means it to be, there is power there to correct, to restore, and to enlarge it.

If any group of Christians who claim to believe and practice all God has said in His Book will face up to their personal responsibility within the family of Christ, and to the real needs of Christians around them, their church will impress its community with the shining goodness of God's love — to them *and* among them.

Such a transformation probably would do more to attract others to Jesus Christ than any house-to-house canvass, evangelistic campaign, or new church facility. People are hungry for acceptance, love, and friends, and unless they find them in the church they may not stay there long enough to become personally related to Jesus Christ.

This chapter has challenged you to think honestly about your general attitude toward people, especially other Christians. The next chapter will dare you to examine your feelings about certain people in particular: The *Ins* and the *Outs* and people who are different from other Christians in some way — in appearance, intellect, tastes, opinions, or practices.

6

INS, OUTS, AND DIFFERENTS

It's easy to subscribe to the idea of loving Christians in general, but most of us have trouble with certain individuals:

> To dwell above
> With saints we love—
>   Oh, that will be glory!
> To live below
> With saints we know —
>   That's another story![1]

Let's return to the convenient terms I defined at the close of Chapter 1 — the *Ins* and the *Outs*. Do you experience special feelings in your contacts with certain individuals in your local church group who are better looking and better dressed than you are, or more talented, successful, prosperous, or popular? And do you fall prey to another set of carnal feelings when confronted with acquaintances who are less good looking, talented, successful, prosperous, or popular than you are?

We saw in Chapter 5 that we should accept and love other Christians as God does — without discrimination. In this connection, it's healthy to do some thinking about special situations we meet in our churches.

Even though Christians ought not to feel class-conscious — either superior or inferior to others — at times these feelings come to most of us, and we need to face them honestly.

Someone has realistically divided a local congregation into three categories: (1) Those who are satisfied with their personal friends and position in the church and largely indifferent to the needs of those who aren't. (2) Those who reluctantly and listlessly accept a tolerable but unsatisfying relation to the church group. (3) Those who are resentful, resigned, or full of self-pity because of the friends and position they don't have.

Ask yourself honestly which group you belong to.

Look at the Ins

To work out a good attitude toward people who are better accepted than you are, you must begin with your view of yourself. This was discussed in Chapter 4. Let's add here that the basic reason why you resent the *Ins* may be not so much that they are snobbish as that you have a low view of yourself. Perhaps you measure yourself by what others think you are, rather than by what you know yourself to be.

When you care enough about what you are (as a person and as a Christian) to become, with God's help, what you *ought* to be, then you can fully respect and love yourself and not wilt under the dazzling success of the *In* people. If you have a personal problem in this area, Chapter 8 is especially for you.

It's human to try to account for the greater popularity of some people by believing that they *tried* to get ahead of you, that they schemed and maneuvered themselves into social acceptance and positions of responsibility and honor. But be fair! There are probably good reasons for their success and general acceptance.

They *are* good looking, or have personal charm, good taste in clothes, or tact and grace, and they *are* outgoing rather than self-conscious in their contacts with people. They are poised, self-confident, often energetic and efficient in their activities; they have good social instincts, are comfortable to be with (if they want to be with you!), and are usually pleasant under stress.

They also may have the advantages of education, cultural
background, wide experience, and leadership ability, business
or professional success and the prosperity it brings. They are
popular because they are attractive, capable, delightful human beings. Be big enough to recognize their worth.
This is, of course, not true of all the *In*-people. Some are
self-centered, aggressive, dominating climbers, determined to
get ahead no matter how, and largely indifferent to those they
pass in their upward climb. But don't suspect *all* well-accepted people of these qualities. Credit them with being
what they are and having done what they have done. This
kind of sincere respect can make room for genuine Christian
love for the folks who seem to be above you — a love they
usually deserve and often need.

Remember, too, that though God has not chosen *many* "wise,
or powerful, or of high social status from the human point of
view,"[2] He *does* choose and often uses, people from the upper classes. He chose Saul of Tarsus — a distinguished member
of the Jewish Sanhedrin — as well as more ordinary men.

Many upper-crust people are being won to Christ today,
and their testimony is impressive because they *are* prominent,
distinguished individuals. And they can reach a class of people we middle-class folks would never reach! God has His
people among the elite, too — and He needs them there.

Their material success enables these Christians to support
the Church and its missionary enterprises in a larger way.
And don't forget that most of them have succeeded because
they are good businessmen and know how to evaluate situations and make wise decisions. Don't try to depreciate them.
Don't suspect their motives and methods because you have had
smaller financial success.

Some Christians complain that only the "big shots" — the
rich and prominent people — are put in positions of authority
in the church. This shouldn't always be true, but often it is
reasonable and right. Such men have executive ability, training, and experience that are valuable to the church when
they're combined with a vital personal relation to Jesus Christ
and thorough dependence on God for direction.

When successful men control the affairs of a local church

without these spiritual qualifications it can spell deterioration, if not disaster, for the work of God in that place. Business know-how and decision-making skills are no substitute for dependence on God.

Before you criticize prosperous Christians for the kind of cars or homes they buy, remember that these deluxe items are often good investments for those who can afford them, and that if you had their bank accounts you might make the very same purchases. Even if you wouldn't, that doesn't prove that they shouldn't.

What is more, large, beautiful homes that are dedicated to Christ can be a great asset to a church as well as in evangelizing the unchurched. Here people can come together in larger numbers and greater comfort than in more modest houses, and the togetherness in a home is hard to duplicate in church facilities.

As for me, the fellowship I experience with God's people has often offered an extra dividend — the pleasure of seeing and enjoying, even for a short time, a large, gracious home. It's a delight to be there, and — since I do my own housework — an equal delight to return to a home that's easier for me to keep in order and pay for!

They're Human, Too

People in the lower social brackets are often quite ready to discuss the *In* people, to evaluate and criticize their way of life and their performance in the church. But I wanted to hear it from someone who was *In*, who was a warm, committed Christian and articulate besides. So I made an appointment with a charming and distinguished Christian friend with the announced purpose of talking with her about how the *In* people feel.

My friend especially wanted other Christians to know that these who seem to be "the chosen people" are simply human beings too. Behind their façade of prosperity and happiness there may be deep needs. They are not always happy (if they are honest about it). They experience many of the same problems less fortunate people have to meet.

A top-bracket pop singer was asked in a television interview what his prescription for happiness was. He answered, "Mister, *I'm* not happy! I'm lonely as hell!" Important people often live under the pressure of gigantic career and social responsibilities. They are surrounded (sometimes almost suffocated) by a host of people who are an inescapable part of their world — people with whom they must maintain some social relationships.

I remember a lovely and well-to-do woman who belonged to one of my home Bible classes. She startled the class one morning by saying that she just didn't have any problems in her life.

But later she told me how, when she drives along a throughway, she sometimes sees in the distance a simple little house, off by itself, surrounded by open country, and says to herself, "How I wish I could live in a plain little home like that for a while — free of the endless complexities and demands that rest on me!" Then she told me something of the multiplied pressures that fill her days, pressures that cloud some of the glamour other women see in her way of life.

Some prominent people are actually lonely for Christian fellowship, especially if their Christian position has cut them off from some other social contacts. Too often we stand in awe of the *Ins* and hesitate to reach out to them even when we are aware of a need in their lives. We leap to the relief of the down-and-outs, but sometimes the up-and-ins are just as needy and we are slower to respond. We foolishly imagine that someone on their own level would be more acceptable, but sometimes none of them respond!

The rich and popular, like the rest of us, have heartaches, temptations (more perhaps), and fears. They may seem blissfully secure socially and economically, but they are walking a tightrope if they live for human approval and applause. They know the fickleness of public approbation. Even among Christians, one's place on the totem pole can suddenly be changed.

Especially among young people, even the most *In* live in a degree of insecurity. They are afraid that for some reason they will lose their favorable position and find themselves "included out."

Lasting popularity spoils some people, gives them a superiority complex and an unconscious contempt for people who don't make their league. Their social acceptance seems to be ready-made.

One father announced that he hoped his daughter wouldn't be beautiful. He believed that those who too easily find acceptance and popularity may never make the effort to become thoroughly likable, deserving individuals. Often those who lack sudden popularity work harder at being kind, friendly, and responsible. They have to *win* affection, and in the long run may be better friends for you than those who automatically attract people.

Another thing to keep in mind about the *In* group, when you view them from outside, is that they may not actually be as intimately related to each other as you imagine.

Life looks like a ball for the *Ins,* "but," says Richards, "it doesn't necessarily feel that way inside."

A Student Council president, a high school fellow working closely with the *In* kids, "the ones that every teen would like to be like — the popular, contented and happy kids," observed, "Someone has to let other teens know that even these kids are not happy and contented, but farther from it than anyone else on the social ladder. They are constantly frustrated within themselves."[3]

Keith Miller recalls how as a youngster, moving from city to city, he envied "groups of boys who seemed to be such close buddies," and wished he could be part of what they seemed to be sharing. But later, when he did become part of such groups and was a leader in several, he was surprised to discover that "except in rare instances, 'in-group' members are not nearly as loving and vulnerable to each other about their real problems and aspirations as they appear to be *from the outside.*" He discovered "the 'façade of intimacy' which in-groups often wear."[4]

Sometimes the most such a clique have in common is their going with the same people to the same places to do the same things at the same time. So don't be too sure that they enjoy rich personal relationships with each other. You may find more rewarding friendships outside their circle.

Remember, too, that well-established leaders in your church group are probably already socially loaded. They have about all the friends and social engagements they can handle, and if they don't include you in their activities it may not be so much because they don't like you as that their lives are already full of people, and there are limits to what one can handle in this area. It's true that they do assimilate a new person now and then, but they are not your best bet if you are reaching out for friends. Some Christians sit and pine because they can't gain admittance to a certain select group when they might better look somewhere else.

Some *In* people, even among Christians, have conspicuous faults, and other Christians (equally aware of their own sterling characters!) react to the *Ins* with a blazing sense of injustice. This is the moment to remember that people don't always get what they deserve or deserve what they get. Many better people never make the grade socially, and some inferior people achieve a larger degree of social importance.

So don't feel necessarily superior if you're *In,* nor inferior if you're not. This is life. But behind the scene there is an all-knowing God who is absolutely just. In the end, His books will balance, and no one who trusts Him more than they trust their own limited ability to evaluate and order life will ever be a loser.

Jesus said, "Those who are last will be first, and those who are first will be last."[5]

One more thing to remember when you look at *Ins* who sometimes are thought (often unfairly) to be snobbish: Snobbery is a sin not confined to the *Ins* in their attitude towards people they consider inferior. Snobbery also includes "one who blatantly imitates, fawningly admires, or vulgarly seeks association with those he regards as his superiors" (Webster). So don't *you* be snobbish!

Ten Commandments for Viewing the Ins

1. Genuinely admire the *Ins* and express (to them and to

others) your appreciation for their service to your church.
They usually deserve respect and recognition.

2. Don't envy them. "Love is not jealous."[6] The distribution of talents and successes is God's business, not yours. Be content with your own lot. "Jealousy is more dangerous and cruel than anger."[7]

Envy Went to Church

Envy went to church this morning.
Being Legion, he sat in every other pew.
Envy fingered wool and silk fabrics,
Hung price tags on suits and neckties.
Envy paced through the parking lot
Scrutinizing chrome and paint.
Envy marched to the chancel with the choir
During the processional. . . .
Envy prodded plain jane wives
And bright wives married to milquetoast dullards,
And kind men married to knife-tongued shrews.
Envy thumped at widows and widowers,
Jabbed and kicked college girls without escorts,
Lighted invisible fires inside khaki jackets.
Envy conferred often this morning
With all of his brothers;
He liked his Sunday scores today
But not enough:
Some of his intended clients
Had sipped an antidote marked Grace,
And wore a moly flower named Love.

— Elva McAllaster*

3. Don't criticize the *Ins*. You might be more like them if you had what it took to get them where they are.

4. Be as ready to love the *Ins* as you are the *Outs*.

5. Show the *Ins* your love and concern in practical, personal ways when you know that they have special needs.

6. Pray for these leaders by name, especially in their responsibilities in the church. Talk about their faults to God rather than to other people.

---

*Reprinted by permission from *Christian Life* magazine, copyright January 1970, Christian Life Publications Inc., Gundersen Drive and Schmale Road, Wheaton, Illinois 60187.

7. Don't assume that they feel unfriendly to you.

8. Cooperate with them in church affairs and projects. Don't label them "a hierarchy of bosses."

9. Don't sell out to win their approval. Some church members are afraid to be themselves or say what they think for fear of getting "out" with the *Ins*. "Giving preferred treatment to rich people is a clear case of selling one's soul for a piece of bread."[8]

When at a church business meeting my husband or I had said what we honestly thought (contrary to another opinion), others would be sure to say to us, after the session, "I'm so glad you said what you did. I think you're right." When we'd ask why they hadn't stood up and said so, there were always excuses. Perhaps they wouldn't risk losing friends. We lost some, but we could still respect ourselves as well as the folks with whom we differed.

10. Live first to please God, not people. When you live for *His* approval, the indifference of men won't be a major calamity.

Look at the Outs

Remember that we defined the *Outs* (for our purposes) as people who are *less* well accepted than the *Ins* but not necessarily friendless or rejected.

Two other terms — "rich" and "poor" — also need explanation, for they appear later in this chapter in quotations from the Bible. "Rich" can mean not only those who have much money, but those who have a big supply of other treasures — personality, success, or friends. "Poor," on the other hand, may also represent people who lack those good things — unimpressive, seemingly unimportant, or inferior people — who are hungry not so much for food as for acceptance, love, and friends.

I'm talking now to you who to some degree feel socially secure. Before you turn to look at folks who seem to be less attractive or successful than you are, and who (for obvious or unknown reasons) are not as well accepted, take a quick look at yourselves. Only as you see yourself clearly can you hope to see others rightly.

You have distinct advantages — your appearance, personality, background, or present situation. "Even his own neighbors despise the poor man, while the rich have many 'friends.' "[9] You may deserve some credit for the success you have achieved, but don't let it go to your head. Listen to what God says: "None of you should be proud of one man and despise the other. Who made you superior to others? *Didn't God give you everything you have?* Well, then, how can you brag, as if what you have were not a gift?"[10]

You will be safe in your high place before men if you stay in a low place before God, accepting your advantages and privileges as from Him and thanking Him for them. There would be less friction between the *Ins* and the *Outs* if both remembered that they are on one level before God. As sinners, they have the same need and God's provision for meeting that need in Christ is the same. He and His resources are available to them both.

Among Christ's disciples and members of the earliest churches, there were few who were great or gifted. Paul wrote to the Corinthians, "God purposely chose . . . what the world looks down on, and despises, and thinks is nothing, in order to destroy what the world thinks is important. This means that not one person can boast in God's presence."[11]

And it is this God who, in the plainest language, condemns conceit and pride among His children:

"I say to all of you: Do not think of yourselves more highly than you should. Instead, be modest in your thinking."[12] Like less prominent people, you battle self, fall into sin, disappoint your Lord, and fail others. See yourself as you know you are, not as admiring people imagine you to be, and you won't so easily feel proud and put on airs.

"Pride goes before destruction and haughtiness before a fall."[13]

"Pride disgusts the Lord."[14]

"There are six things the Lord hates . . . no, seven:"[15] — and guess what comes first in the list. Haughtiness!

"If anyone respects and fears God, he will hate evil."[16]

And which two of the four evils that follow are named first? Pride and arrogance!

If you are superior to others in certain ways, you don't have to pretend — in order to be humble — that you don't have these advantages. But realize that having them doesn't make you any better than those who don't. "Don't do anything from selfish ambition, or from a cheap desire to boast; but be humble toward each other, never thinking you are better than others."[17] You are just *different*.

One who is a fine soloist is no better than someone who can't carry a tune — he is just different. Maybe the unmusical person can cook better, write a poem, pray in faith, or win more people to Christ.

God says it is better to be "poor and humble than proud and rich."[18] In view of how desirable it seems to be rich, it must be terribly important to be humble! If you are *In,* but are cocky, superior, uncaring, or condescending toward the *Outs, they* may be more pleasing to God (if they are humble, content, free of envy and resentment toward the *Ins*) than *you* are!

One man who is a warm, enthusiastic Christian is also unusually intelligent, successful, and self-confident. He often told me how he had achieved exactly what he set out to do in life — became a member of the most distinguished fraternity in his university, graduated with highest honors, won the girl he determined to marry, succeeded in the career he chose, and gained admittance to the most exclusive country club.

He was superior, but even though I'm sure he didn't realize it, his sense of personal superiority came through continually in subtle ways — the smugness in his tone of voice and subtle references to his own good taste, fine performance, and keen discernment. It put a constant strain on his friendships.

A. W. Tozer made this realistic observation: "Pride and arrogance sometimes get into the Church of God, and that's bad, brother! There's that tone of command. Then that superior look. And a superior bearing. Pride and arrogance stick out all the way around.

"Watch out, Christian brothers and sisters, for the danger of arrogance — assuming that you are somebody indeed!

"God will never let you high-hat somebody else if you are a Christian. If you are a Christian, the Lord loves you too much to let you get away with that. You may say: 'What will the Lord do, then, if I get arrogant and presumptuous, full of pride over my victory and success?' Well, the Lord will rebuke you painfully. . . .

"Paul said if any man thinks that he amounts to anything, let him know that he won't amount to anything until he gets over it."[19]

Christians sometimes feel and act superior even when they're not outstandingly good looking, successful career-wise, or rich. They suffer from *spiritual* pride. They look down on another Christian because he doesn't always go to prayer meeting, or lead in public prayer when he does go. Or he hasn't been "filled" with the Holy Spirit, spoken in tongues, or quit smoking.

This is the worst form of snobbery. Whether or not these "superior" folks can claim to be *In* with people, they let it be known that they do have a special *In* with God, and that many other Christians are just not in their class.

Their smugness often grows out of negative positions — they are "separated" Christians because they don't indulge in certain questionable amusements or habits: they are proudly "separated" from affiliation with all other Christians who don't see eye-to-eye with them on the correct form of baptism, the details of future events prophesied in the Bible, church organization, or the policies of Billy Graham.

There's nothing wrong with being strongly convinced about all of these matters, but — especially where the Bible has left room for difference of opinion — there is something wrong when you look down on doctrinally sound Christians who don't agree with you on some detail and yet are equally sincere in their desire to please God.

After all, since there are multitudes of regenerate Christians on both sides of some issues, and since we are going to spend a long eternity with them in the same place, perhaps we had better start accepting and respecting *and loving* each other in this life to get ready for the next.

Problem People

Some Christians fall into sin — immorality or worldliness. Whatever your own or your church's view of discipline may be, remember that these people are to be treated with loving concern, not contempt or a holier-than-thou attitude. You can let them know you love them and care about them without approving what they have done. Above all, don't show your disapproval as some Christians do by snubbing them or gossiping about them.

Trouble between Christians may grow out of friction rather than moral misconduct. Paul asked two women in the Philippian church, "I beg you . . . to make up your differences as Christians should."[20]

How do you react to the program chairman of the Women's Fellowship when she fails to meet her responsibility and the business falls on your already loaded shoulders as president? To the dogmatic deacon who declares that anyone who goes to movies isn't fit to join the church? Or to the church members who go? To that man who had the nerve to speak against the Board's recommendation that the church build an impressive sanctuary because he sincerely believed that Christian education facilities were more needed? To girls who wear their skirts short, guys who wear their hair long, or those over-30's who show their disapproval of both? To that retarded boy who doesn't fit into any part of the youth program but insists on coming?

Is your Christian love virile enough to include all of these? They're not excluded from God's love. Are they from yours?

Some Christians are not so much objectionable as just too different to be welcome in the church family. There's that home Bible study bunch who are investigating charismatic gifts — speaking in tongues and healing. And the woman who writes poetry (and sells it!) and belongs to a Great Books Club. Then there's that bookworm teen-ager who is accused of using big words to impress people. (His language is simply the result of his wide reading.)

Perhaps you boast that you have no racial prejudice, but you don't know quite how to feel about that black couple who want to join the church. They have young people who would be in the youth group and might want to date your kids. And then there's that young lawyer who claims to be a Christian but doesn't vote the Republican ticket!

Do you feel love for these folks, or do you view them with disapproval (almost disgust) and find veiled ways to let them know how you feel?

A mother whose daughter has had emotional problems wrote me: "In school Debbie (fictitious name) didn't have much ability to make friends, so felt left out. You know how cruel children can be to someone who is different. She has been bitter about their treatment of her. . . . Do you think she will be lonely in heaven? So many people you meet in the world and in the church are cold and uncaring. . . . Yes, you may use my letters in your book, as you asked. Maybe it will cause someone not to be too hard on those who are different."

It's hard for the scrupulous Christian (called the "weaker" brother by the Apostle Paul)[21] to accept Christians who find freedom in Christ to do some things the weaker brother feels he shouldn't do. Because there is room for a difference of opinion in some matters of Christian conduct (not in basic doctrine), the stricter brother must learn to accept and love the one who enjoys more freedom in Christ.

But perhaps the biggest order is for the Christian who has "knowledge" (or freedom) to accept and love — and show consideration for — the brother who is bound and circumscribed unnecessarily by his over-scrupulous conscience.

Such mutual tolerance and consideration is God's plan for personal relationships among His people. Yet too often Christians condemn and despise each other instead of accepting the other's right to get individual leading from God in debatable areas.

Remember too, as you review the great variety of individuals in your church, that God often uses for His own purposes seemingly strange, nonconformist individuals. John the Baptist — with his rough camel's hair clothes and diet of locusts and honey — was one of them.

Today He often uses outspoken, forward-thinking individuals who are nonconformists in many areas of Christian

action — personal appearance, church music, Christian education, soul-winning, foreign mission projects, youth work. Are
you who are the "pillars of the church" able to accept church
members (and voters!) you can't control? Such independent,
nonparty people may threaten the *status quo,* but they just
may be the key to church renewal. In any case, because of
their independence they may lack or lose friends in their
churches.

So, you *Ins* (and all who look down on anyone), take an
honest look before God at your personal attitudes toward other
Christians — people who are largely overlooked, unattractive,
provoking, objectionable, more (or less) finicky than yourselves about questionable practices, retarded or highly intellectual, who wear too much makeup or not enough, whose
skirts are too long or too short, whose faces are buried in
beards or whose old-fashioned crew cuts make them look like
"peeled onions"!

Let God enlarge your heart to hold them all.

And then ask Him to extend your heart's dimensions so
that you can also relate in brotherly love to people who are as
warmly devoted to Jesus Christ as you are but who differ
with you about some minor doctrinal or organizational matters
on which the Bible is not perfectly clear — the length of time
in which God created the world, the exact time relation of the
Rapture of the Church to the Tribulation, divine healing or
speaking in tongues, dispensational details, or the structure of
church government.

No matter how strong your personal convictions may be on
such matters, never look down on these sincere, Bible-believ-
ing brothers or view them as religious *Outs.* Allow them their
personal right even to be wrong in some opinion (you could
be too!) and retain your respect and love for them as fellow
Christians.

My husband and I are often involved in meetings, confer-
ences, or retreats for Christians of one denomination or another, or of interdenominational character. How we relish the
fellowship with believers of many different labels! It's exciting
and inspiring to realize that in spite of minor differences we
belong to each other as well as to Jesus Christ. There is good-

ness and sweetness there that surpasses even the richest relationships within a single group or denomination.

We don't urge the end of divisions and the setting up of one ecumenical union, but Christians should be able to love all true believers across denominational lines and enjoy their essential oneness in Christ.

Ten Commandments for Viewing the Outs

1. If you are *In,* remember that your position means responsibility as well as privilege. "The man to whom much is given, of him much is required; the man to whom more is given, of him much more is required."[22] You will have to give account to God for what you have done with the position and possessions He gave you.

2. Ask God to keep you humble. Paul counted "as complete loss" his own impressive, prestigious background and accomplishments for what he called "so much more valuable, the knowledge of Christ Jesus my Lord. . . . For his sake," he wrote, "I have thrown everything away."[23] Remember that all of us — *Ins* and *Outs* — were once *Out* with God but are now *In* with Him because of Jesus' redeeming work.[24]

3. Try to understand people who feel unaccepted, lonely, left out — even when reasons for their unpopularity are visible. Newspaper columnist Sydney Harris says that a saint is one who can *identify* with a dissimilar. It isn't enough to accept people who are different, or seem inferior. Try to stand in their shoes and face their problems and limitations.

Ed McMahon, telling about his lonely, friendless childhood says, "It was just awful." Moving from town to town he was never able to settle in one place long enough to have a hometown or a neighborhood gang of friends. "I wanted to go out for football," he recalls, "but when I went to practice, all the guys were slapping one another on the back and shoving one another around, and I sat there on the bench alone. I gave up going out for football. It's a terrible feeling for a kid to feel so out of it." Jesus reacted to needy people with compassion. Do you?

4. No matter how relatively *Out* some Christians may seem

to be, treat them as equals, which they are in Christ. The thoroughly delightful custodian of a large evangelical church told me how much he and his wife valued the friendship of the few people in the church who treated them as equals rather than as inferiors. Christian considerations aside, it is said that most of those whom the world considers to be truly great treat their inferiors as equals.

5. Appreciate the faithfulness and service of less prominent Christians, and let them (and others) *know* that you do. Some who can't teach are Sunday school secretaries, choir members, refreshment servers, altar boys, reliable baby sitters. Some distinguish themselves by being faithful in attendance at services, praying for the needs of the church and individuals in it, or greeting strangers and being friendly to everyone. Such people may be inconspicuous but are invaluable.

6. Remember that less successful people meet the same problems you meet (and some you don't) but often have more limited resources with which to meet them. Show that you are personally concerned, and offer practical, loving help. "Command those who are rich in the things of this life not to be proud . . . to do good, to be rich in good works, to be generous and ready to share with others."[25]

7. Take a personal stand against exclusiveness, cliquishness, and snobbery as completely contrary to Christian standards. Speak out (you Christian young people especially) against mocking, ridiculing, excluding, and persecuting others. If you are well accepted, you have special responsibility in this area because the *Outs* won't dare to do it. And if you're really a leader in your group the rest are likely to respect your opinions. Let those opinions count for Christ. "It's nice to be important, but it's more important to be nice!"[26]

8. Share yourself and something of your own needs with folks who may feel that they are inferior to you or are not as well accepted in your church. Ask them to pray for you. This will do more to bridge the gap between you than your offering to help them, and you'll get strong prayer support, too.

9. Never lose sight of the real possibility of moral and spiritual disaster in the lives of people who feel unwanted or

friendless in your church. They may leave it to find friends elsewhere, and may get involved with religious groups that offer little spiritual help or actually dispense false teaching. Others who leave simply dismiss the church as not for them, and categorically reject Christ because of the unfriendliness of the people who represent Him.

10. Don't imagine that everyone who seems to be less *In* than you are would like to change places with you. Many prefer their simpler, less complicated way of life and may have found a measure of contentment and fulfilment unknown to you. There's always the possibility that if you could look inside their personal lives and their relation to God, you might find reason to *envy* them.

7

GIVE YOURSELF AWAY

Which is more important to you — being *in* with the right people or being "great" in the eyes of God?

Someone has put it squarely: How popular you were among men may affect the number of people at your funeral, but by then the only thing you'll care about will be what *God* thinks of you. And God has made it clear that His standard of greatness doesn't coincide with man's idea of personal success.

When Jesus' disciples were quarreling over who should be greatest in the Kingdom, Jesus told them, "You know that the rulers of the people have power over them, and the leaders rule over them. This, however, is not the way it shall be among *you. If one of you wants to be great, he must be the servant of the rest;* and if one of you wants to be first, he must be your slave — like the Son of Man, who *did not come to be served, but to serve.*"[1] Jesus wasn't talking about how to become a Christian or get rid of your sins. He was talking to those who already were His followers about how to distinguish themselves in His sight.

The Church of Jesus Christ would be transformed overnight if every Christian would honestly sort out his life goals. What are we really concerned about — the impression we make on people or the impression we make on God?

Even the early Christians had problems in this area. When

Paul was desperately concerned about the Christians at Philippi, he wrote that he hoped to send Timothy soon to bring back news of them. "He is the only one who shares my feelings, and who really cares about you," he told them. "All the others seem to be wrapped up in their own affairs, and do not really care for the business of Jesus Christ."[2]

Our "own affairs" — going to school, earning a living, keeping a home, raising children — rightly require a large amount of our time and energy and are a large part of the "business" God has assigned us. But we still find time for other things that are important to us.

How eager are you to be one of the "great" ones in God's family — great because you give yourself away, freely and gladly, to serve Him and His people? In our particular circle of Christians each of us is to be "the servant of the rest."

Let's look beyond the general attitude of Christians toward each other (Chapter 5) to specific, practical ways in which individual Christians can serve each other. And please remember that although Christians should and do give themselves in loving service to people outside the Church as well as in it, we are here mostly concerned with problems of personal relationship within a local church. What *the Church* can do will be the subject of Chapter 9.

"But I Don't Want To!"

Living to serve others isn't a popular idea today because it's diametrically opposed to human nature. We instinctively look out for ourselves and like to feel that it's up to others to do the same for themselves. To give ourselves consistently to others is to experience a complete change of direction quite beyond the reach of most of us apart from the power of Jesus Christ at work in us.

He set the example: "Look out for each other's interests, not just for your own. The attitude you should have is the one Christ Jesus had: He always had the very nature of God, but . . . of his own free will he gave it all up and took the nature of a servant. He became like man. . . . He was humble and walked the path of obedience to death — his death on the cross." By this stooping, Jesus rescued a lost race, and "for this reason God raised him to the highest place above, and gave him the name that is greater than any other name."[3]

Of course no Christian can do everything that needs doing. But do we sometimes feel too fine or too important or too busy to offer the simple, humble, even menial help that would put a rainbow in another Christian's clouded sky?

On the very threshold of His crucifixion and soon-coming ascension, the Lord Jesus, in concern that His followers should be ready to provide for each other's personal and practical needs, gave them a startling demonstration.

Taking off His outer garment, He "tied a towel around his waist . . . poured some water into a washbasin, and began to wash his disciples' feet and dry them with the towel around his waist." After He had washed their feet Jesus returned to His place at the table.

" 'Do you understand what I have just done to you?' " He asked. " 'You call me Teacher and Lord, and it is right that you do so, because I am. I am your Lord and Teacher, and I have just washed your feet. *You, then, should wash each other's feet.* I have set an example for you, so that you will do just what I have done for you. I tell you the truth: no slave is greater than his master; and no messenger is greater than the one who sent him.' "[4]

Have you stooped as Jesus did to minister in simple, practical ways to the Christians you know?

Jesus is so great because He stooped so low. He had to choose between doing His own will or His Father's will, and it was no easy decision. As He wrestled with the choice the night before His crucifixion, "His sweat was like drops of blood falling to the ground." But in that awful hour He surrendered to His Father's purpose: "Not my will . . . but your will be done."[5] Doing the will of God meant sacrificing Himself, setting aside self-protection, and exposing Himself to infinite suffering for desperately needy but utterly unworthy people.

Does your will — what *you* want out of life, what you want to be and do — get in the way of humbly serving the needs of those whose lives you touch? Perhaps before you can give yourself away to others for Christ's sake you need to settle the conflict between your will and His will. It won't be an easy decision, but it can be the most exciting and productive one you will ever make. It will radically change your personal relationships at home, at school, at the office, in the neighborhood, and to the members of your church.

One reason the Church is not famous today for the quality of its internal love is that so many Christians have never settled this important matter.

If you're looking for a change of pace and real adventure — try this. Live not to be waited on and paid attention to, but to serve others. Meet people with your antenna out — sensitive to their situation and their personal need, and ready to do anything you can to meet that need. Don't depend too largely on the pastor's sermon or the deacon's relief fund to solve their individual problems.

"I Care About You"

"The power of the personal is the power to hear and to help one another, and, incidentally, to be heard and helped ourselves — the power to live together with mutual help and creativeness."[6]

Paul wrote to the young Thessalonian church, "Because of our love for you we were ready to share with you not only the Good News from God, but *even our own lives.* You were so dear to us!"[7] Those persecuted Christians knew the apostle cared about them!

Sometimes you can't give much more than a sincere, brief, personal word to someone. But often that's just what he needs — the assurance that somebody cares.

Hurrying along the main street of our town one day, I met a friend. I was pressured for time, and consciously told myself I couldn't stop to talk. But something held me, and I asked her how things were in her world. She told me about a serious crisis that had arisen in her family, and I promised to pray about it. When I called back later, she added this to her report:

"Marion, thank you for calling. We asked the folks in our church to pray with us about this, but only two people in the whole church have inquired about it since!" And I wouldn't even have known if I hadn't taken that minute on Main Street. Burkhart tells of a seminary professor of pastoral counseling who said, "After a student says, 'I need to see you,' I say, 'I want to see you, but my schedule is full until Tuesday at 4:00.' Occasionally, when the time comes, the student arrives and says, 'I guess I don't need to see you; I got it worked out on my own.' "

"Why?" asks Burkhart. "The professor cared. For a moment the young man wasn't alone; for a bit he was in the circle of loving concern. It was enough. Then he could go it alone."[8]

But it's not enough to care. Let the person *know* you care about him.

Jacob Loewen tells about a first-grader named Billy, whose family were Christians and were making a special study of how to tell others about Christ. At about the same time the father of Jim, one of Billy's classmates, was killed in a tractor accident. Billy prayed for his classmate every day.

One day at school Billy walked downstairs with Jim, determined to tell him about Jesus. "How are you getting along?" Billy began.

Jim smiled and said, "Fine, just fine."

Billy continued, "Do you know I've been praying for you every day since your daddy got killed?"

The other little fellow grabbed Billy's hand and took him behind the school building. "That was a lie when I said things are going fine; they aren't fine. We are having trouble with the cows and with the machines. My mother doesn't know what to do. But I didn't know that you were praying for me."[9]

People will be slow to share their real needs unless they understand that you are open to them and concerned about them. If you're genuinely interested in them, it won't be hard to let them know it, but a pretended concern will get little response.

Do you feel special compassion for needy people who don't have friends, are unattractive or even physically repulsive and likely to be left out by others?

Jesus' parable of the Good Samaritan points up the fact that the man who was robbed and beaten found himself in a situation where there was no one to help — no family or friends. The strangers who passed by reacted only by looking away from the unpleasant sight of a man "half dead." But when the good Samaritan passed that way, "his heart was filled with pity." Because he felt compassion rather than revulsion, he did what was necessary to meet the man's need.[10]

I know a Christian woman who is charming and well dressed and who holds a responsible position in a business firm, but who has not considered herself too high-class or too busy to take personal, long-range interest in individual Christians who have been rejected or overlooked by other members of her church.

Three examples: One, a young woman who had a mental breakdown and was for years a patient in a mental hospital. Another, an eccentric but needy woman of another nationality, with whom my friend has lunch regularly. Third, a family where the children were victims of alcoholic parents.

Rather than being degraded by such personal relationships, my friend stands high in the respect and love of those who know her.

When Paul was in prison in Rome, Onesiphorus came to visit him. This was Paul's report of his friend's arrival: "He was not ashamed that I am in prison, but as soon as he arrived in Rome he started looking for me until he found me."[11]

How many "prisoners" — lonely, rejected, shut-out folks — are you unashamed to bring within the circle of your friendship?

Christians today may find themselves "jailed" in a bad marriage. Young people often feel shut out of their parents' love and concern, and some are rejected for their faith by non-Christian parents. Others feel unwanted at church because they adopt dress or hair styles some Christians disapprove. Elderly people may be physically shut into the four walls of a house or nursing home. Those who take care of small children or sick folks may feel as shut in as those they take care of. Disfigured or handicapped people often feel socially exiled. Can you help meet any of these needs?

When Jesus walked on the water in the storm, He changed His course and got into the storm-tossed boat with His disciples.

He not only recognized their need but exposed Himself to its danger. He became involved.[12]

Love in Action

"My children! Our love should not be just words and talk; it must be true love, which shows itself in action."[13] "Show your love by being helpful to one another."[14]

When the evangelical church teaches that you are saved by faith in Christ, not by good works, does it mean that a Christian is not to be concerned about doing good? Is he less interested in it than a "religious" man who is trying to earn his way into heaven?

"It is by God's grace that you have been saved, through faith. It is not your own doing, but God's gift . . . not the result of your own efforts. God . . . *has created us for a life of good works.*"[15]

Why did Jesus die for us? "To rescue us from all wickedness and make us a people who belong to him alone and are *eager to do good.*"[16] Are you eager? Or only glad to be bound for heaven?

The rest of this chapter will suggest a wide range of specific, down-to-earth ways in which we can "do good," especially in meeting the needs of other Christians. But before you say it, let me acknowledge that there are real limits to what one individual Christian can do. We can't do everything we'd like to do or that needs to be done. There are human limits to helpful loving. We are limited by our strength and by our other responsibilities. There are also limits that discretion puts on us, like the help one may want to offer to someone of the opposite sex.

I remember Lillian Weaver's answer to a question about a Christian's inability to meet all the needs of which he becomes aware. She pictured Christians as walking along the road of life with people in every direction reaching out their hands for help of one kind or another. "You can't help them all," she admitted, "but you can give yourself to those outstretched hands nearest you. Accept *them* as your responsibility." Put

your confidence in God's arranging your life and bringing you
into touch with those He means you to reach.

> I am only one
> But I am one.
> I can't do everything
> But I can do something.
> What I can do
> I ought to do
> And by God's grace
> I shall do.[17]

Here are a few of the "somethings" we can do. They are
part of my experience and the experience of other Christians
whose actions have been prompted by love. You will be able
to add many more.

Learn to pay attention to people. Psychiatrist Donald E.
Smith, writing on "The Healing Touch of Attention," says,
"The person most likely to get results [in helping troubled
people] is the one who has mastered the art of paying attention
— *really* paying attention. . . . Each of us has woven into the
fabric of his being a yearning for attention. Absence of it is a
psychic pain few can endure. . . . All to some extent are voic-
ing the same despairing cry: *Pay attention to me!* . . . Rejection hurts. Attention heals. It is as simple as that."

The first two among his suggestions as to what an average
person can do to increase his skill in this sensitive and often
neglected art are these:

"Learn to listen deeply. The art of paying attention involves
stretching out your mind and heart and focusing on the other
person with all the intensity and awareness that you can command.

"Teach your ego to hold its breath. All of us are self-
centered much of the time. Each of us is an actor trying to
impress an audience, to take the center of the stage. But if
you want to pay close attention to another human being, you
must train your own attention-hungry ego to stop striving for
the spotlight and let it fall on the other person. We have a
name for people who fail consistently to do this; we call them
bores."[18]

This art of paying attention is desperately needed among Christians.

As you become aware of the glad and sad feelings a person is experiencing, let him know that you share what he feels. "Rejoice with those who rejoice, weep with those who weep."[19] "If one part of the body [of Christ] suffers, all the other parts suffer with it; if one part is praised, all the other parts share its happiness."[20]

Think of someone in your world who is happy about something today and let him know that you are happy about it, too. Now think of someone who is distressed or sad — and get word to him that you share his anxiety or sorrow.

Encourage Somebody

If you read a modern translation of the Bible, you will see how often God's people are to encourage one another. Perhaps there is nothing on the human side that people need more than encouragement.

"The one who speaks God's message speaks to men, and gives them help, encouragement, and comfort."[21]

"Anxious hearts are very heavy, but a word of encouragement does wonders!"[22]

"They strengthened the believers and encouraged them to remain true to the faith."[23] Many who defect from the faith today might have remained true if a few individual Christians had offered them reinforcement and encouragement in the face of testing and temptation.

"We must always aim at those things that bring peace, and that help strengthen one another."[24] You can help strengthen a fellow Christian for his particular battle in life — unemployment, rebellious children, sickness, or whatever may come.

Sometimes people need you *after* the battle, whether they won or lost it. "As Abraham was coming back from the battle . . . Melchizedek met him and blessed him."[25]

I remember telephoning a woman who had had major surgery that showed extensive malignancy. I hadn't known about it until she had been home from the hospital for a while.

After apologizing for probably being one of the last to show my concern, I said I was glad she was over the worst of it.

Then she told me that actually she was going through an even more difficult experience now as, knowing her condition, she tried to face the future without depression. She assured me that my call wasn't too late, and asked me to keep praying.

Sometimes, when a loved one has died, the hardest time is sometime afterward. Pastor and friends rally at the hour of crisis, but after the excitement and stress has subsided the full impact of the blow is more fully felt. Then, perhaps more than at first, your loving concern and practical help may be needed.

You can encourage another Christian when he simply needs reassurance. Young people are especially uncertain of themselves as persons and as Christians. Offer a friendly word or an honest expression of approval of what they are or have done. Appreciate their filling a place of service in the church, or praise them for being on the honor roll or the football team, or in the band at school. (You may have to read your local paper carefully to learn when to do this!)

Parents need reassurance about their children. I remember the day when a neighbor for whom my 15-year-old daughter did baby-sitting told me how impressed she was with my daughter's poise! Another startled me by remarking on how mature Lorraine seemed! This was reassurance I could use just then!

Everyone can use a little reassurance about his own person, too. Tell folks when you honestly like their clothes or hairdos; compliment them for being smiling and friendly, for sharing an interesting experience, for presiding, teaching, or singing well, or for the word of encouragement that gave you a needed lift. If you don't have a chance to say it in person, write or telephone.

In all your effort to encourage and help other Christians, be gentle. Paul wrote about his ministry to the Thessalonians, "We were gentle when we were with you, as gentle as a mother taking care of her children. . . . We treated each one of you just as a father treats his own children. We encouraged you, we comforted you."[26]

Who have you encouraged during the past week? Who will you encourage today?

Go Visiting

Make a personal visit when the Lord lays a special need on your heart. Call on new people who have visited your church, on people who are sick or shut in or where there has been a death in the family.

One thing I learned in my fourteen years as a pastor's assistant: when you call on a person whose loved one has died, don't frantically try to avoid talking about him unless there's something gruesome or embarrassing about the death. Even then, the bereaved one may feel a need to talk about it.

Under normal circumstances, tell the happy, interesting, or even humorous things you enjoy remembering about the one who has gone. And often you'll listen while your friend shares his own pleasant memories.

You are not under obligation to take a gift to someone in the hospital, but I was touched and pleased at the assortment of little gifts friends — even mere acquaintances — brought when they visited me there: a cake of sweet-smelling soap, a single flower from their garden, a book to read (and return), candy to share with my nurses, notes for thank-yous, and of course the proverbial dusting powder. In some way this let me know they cared, and I recovered with a new sense of being cherished.

Don't forget to call on sick children and young people. And the smallest gift will put a rainbow over your visit to a child.

Children sometimes come down with long-lasting physical calamities — rheumatic fever or broken bones — and it's hard for an active youngster to stay in bed or wear a cast for weeks or months. A Sunshine Basket can be a boon to his weary parents as well as to the ailing child.

Years ago I decorated the handle of a wicker basket with gay artificial flowers and I have used it (after it has been returned) over and over for this purpose. Get the members of the child's Sunday school class and friends of his parents to contribute gifts. (I have sometimes bought all the gifts myself and used some of my tithe to foot the bill. It is done for God's child and for His sake.)

Inexpensive things can help fill a sick child's long hours — a fresh spool of Scotch tape, a bunch of brightly colored rubber bands, paper dolls, coloring books and crayons, sewing cards, a package of colored construction paper, beads to string, model cars to make, bubble gum, a few lollipops, puzzles, activity books, games, books to read, a package of small plastic figures (farm, Indian, or military), etc.

Insist that the recipient open only one package each day. This project is supposed to supply long-range cheer, but it is useless if all the gifts are opened at once.

I even made a Sunshine Basket for my husband's mother when she was eighty and hospitalized after an accident. She loved it!

Sometimes, when you are going to make a call, invite someone to go with you, even if he's not a close friend of the one you visit. You will have (and be) company en route and you will bring another person into the act of helping.

If you plan to make a call in a home, a phone call in advance will save them (and you) possible embarrassment if they or their house are not prepared for visitors. If they are not at home, it will save you a fruitless trip.

When you meet new people at church, call on them the following week, if you can, or invite them to your home along with a few other people they might enjoy. If visitors at church ask how to find the classes they and their children should be in, don't *tell* them; *take* them to those classrooms and introduce each to the teachers.

I remember our first Sunday in Arizona. A couple we hadn't met before took us out to dinner after the church service! We were touched that anyone would do this for complete strangers, and we felt the warmth of the love for Christ that brought us together with these new friends.

Be sensitive not only to the need of strangers, but to individuals or couples who may have been attending your church for some time but are still unassimilated, who are like an island isolated in a sea of people.

"Solitude is never greater or more painful than in our large cities," says Lepp. "Nowhere, in fact, is man more totally and more painfully alone than in a crowd."[27] And that crowd can be inside the four walls of a Christian church. Perhaps it's even more painful there because it's more out of place.

For a young person to experience such aloneness among his peers there can be a destroying agony, and it sometimes happens. The loner is left to himself, even though his isolation is perfectly visible to all. No one sits with him or talks to him or eats with him, and if he makes any advances he is met with coolness, if not contempt. Any *Ins* who sense his need may be afraid to pay attention to him for fear their friends will disapprove and turn against them. Only the most rugged individual will come back for more after such treatment.

But thoughtless or selfish adults are sometimes just as merciless. A girl who worked for a large Christian organization observed, "The workers in my office are some snobs! They never ask me to go to coffee break with them. I guess I don't really belong to any of their special groups, but I wish that just once in a while they'd include me. I dread going to coffee break alone all the time!"

My husband taught the adults in a vacation Bible school one summer recently. It was a two-period session with time for refreshments between. I noticed that one of the women in his class brought drinks in to any who were not able to go to the refreshment room. One was a crippled woman who stayed in her seat between the sessions. Another was the teacher, who was busy erasing or refilling his chalkboard for the next period. And one night I was another one.

When I commented on her thoughtful concern for others, she told me that she couldn't have anything with sugar in it and that this ruled out all the refreshments available. So she had decided to use the intermission to look after other folks. Even a few selfless individuals of her kind can be a tremendous asset to a church. Forgetting what she might want for herself, she was busy giving herself — along with the Koolaid — to others.

There are bird watchers, girl watchers, and weight watchers. Try being a watcher yourself — keeping an eye out for individuals who need a little friendly loving. Give yourself to them. Sit with them, talk to them, help them to feel included — part of the warm fellowship of your group of Christians.

Take a Meal

Take a meal into a home when it's needed. This is one of the happiest things I do. When the woman of the house is sick, meal-getting falls on the husband and children, who are largely inefficient in this area.

While a mother is in the hospital, invite the rest of the family to your home for a meal. But when the patient first gets home — that's the real crisis. The abandoned family may have scrounged food well enough to keep them alive, but with a helpless convalescent in the picture, good meals are more important.

Let the family know well in advance that the meal is coming and what time it will arrive, and don't always take a casserole!

When possible, take the food in disposable containers. But I'll never forget the festive Christmas dinner that arrived when my husband and I were both sick at the same time. There were silver and crystal containers, a Christmas candle, holly and tinsel, and a small glamour-wrapped gift for each member of the family. I also remember the tears that came when I saw this expression of shining love from a fellow Christian who wasn't even a close friend. That fact made it all the sweeter and made the act a symbol of her loving concern for all who are part of the body of Christ.

Colleen Townsend Evans tells how one summer God convicted her of harboring resentment against certain women she just didn't like or who had done things that hurt her. Her only retaliation had been avoiding them and keeping her resentment inside.

When God showed her that it is real sin to be sensitive about oneself, she wrote down the names of these people and started taking God's Word literally by praying for them: "Love your enemies, and pray for those who mistreat you."[28]

"This," she reports, "led me to do the strangest things for these people. If I baked a pie, I baked two and took one to them. You should have seen the astonished looks on their faces. I would go up to them and for no reason say, 'Here!' They would look at me as if I had two heads or something. But what a miracle God started to work, not because *they* had changed, but because *I* had changed.

"God has shown me that all my problems are not *out there,* but *in here.* How wonderful to find that some of your enemies can become your closest friends."[29]

Such simple acts of kindness carry with them the very fragrance of Christian loving. I remember one particularly demanding weekend when a church friend appeared at my door for no special reason with a loaf of homemade bread, and the same day a neighbor brought in some cupcakes. On birthdays and Christmases you can explain these friendly gestures, but when they happen just *any* day? That's when you feel it, and your smile is inside as well as out.

Write to needy folks who are beyond physical reach. Greeting cards are fine, but their impact is tripled if you add a personal note. If you want to include a Bible verse, don't just print the reference. Copy out the verse, unless you want to give the impression that your time is more valuable than the person's to whom you send the card!

Send local news that will be of interest, but remember to tell your friend about yourself. That's what he most wants to know.

Don't be afraid to put into words your affection for another Christian. Say it or write it, but let him know that you still love him and miss him.

Paul did this repeatedly: "My brothers . . . how dear you are to me, and how I miss you! How happy you make me, and how proud I am of you!"[30] Don't be impersonal and detached. Give yourself in open affection to God's people.

If you have the time, and God leads you in this direction, offer to do some Bible study with a new Christian. Decide together when, where, and how often you will meet for this study, which can do much to establish one who is beginning to walk in God's way. Don't plan on lecture-type teaching, but come together to share what each of you finds in a passage of Scripture. Pray together about what you learn and about your personal needs.

Do you serve other Christians with your car? Children whose parents won't take them to Sunday school can get there in yours. Other folks who don't have automobiles may need a ride to and from church.

Years ago I regularly picked up, for our monthly women's circle meetings, a perky little old lady I might never have known otherwise. We have felt, ever since, that we belong to each other in a special way.

If you find yourself taxiing your own and other parents' young people all over creation for youth activities, don't complain about it. This is another opportunity to use your car to serve.

One mother I knew had a number of teens of her own and constantly ferried them and their friends to varying destinations. I complimented her one day for this ministry (she often transported my daughter along with the others), and she replied that she couldn't teach a Sunday school class or take on leadership in other areas, but that she felt this was something the Lord had given her to do. She enjoyed it thoroughly.

I don't know whether or not other parents thanked her, but on one trip our girl took her a box of chocolates. Don't take such generous services for granted, but express your appreciation.

Your car can also furnish a lot of pleasure to folks who don't get out often. On some necessary trips I have taken with me a boy restricted by rheumatic fever or elderly folks who are usually house-bound. Especially at Christmas-shopping time, I sometimes take along an I-don't-drive friend, let her loose at the beginning of the day, and pick her up at the appointed time for the return trip.

With either the old folks or a young person, I often stop for a "treat," which gives me an excuse for not counting calories!

So don't take your car for granted. Some folks don't have one, some can't drive one. Let your Christian loving play a part in the use of your car. If you're the one who's served, be thankful, and take a turn at paying for the treat!

Some mothers who have a car also have a preschooler who is a temporary but sizable shopping handicap! If you could keep the little one even one morning a month you might supply the harried mother with wings for that morning.

Some Christians are especially sensitive to a person's need for rest and relief. They take over a preschooler after lunch so a convalescing mother can get the afternoon rest she needs. Or they go to a home where someone is sick to take over while a mother, who has been up all night with the patient, can catch up on sleep.

Or they look after the little ones so a mother can get away to visit her sick husband in the hospital. Or they keep one of the children (and arrange places for the others) so that the pastor and his wife can go off unhampered for a few days of much-needed relaxation.

Most people can afford to hire babysitters, but there are times when a sitter isn't available. I remember a woman who once told me that if I were ever hard-put for a sitter, I should feel free to ask her, though under ordinary circumstances she wouldn't be available. Once, when I needed her desperately, I was grateful for her emergency help.

If you can't take on more frequent babysitting, you might offer to come once a month to stay with your pastor's or a missionary's children or to relieve someone who is financially limited.

When I taught a class of young business women they agreed to do volunteer babysitting for our pastor's family and help free him and his wife for the many activities that required their presence.

Old Folks at Home

I have gotten special pleasure from giving myself to elderly people who are geographically near enough so I can run in often even if I can't stay too long.

I don't have to worry about what to talk about. Because they are largely restricted in what they can do, their present lives are uneventful, but they love to retell what happened to them in the past. The folks they live with really don't want to hear their story all over again, and you haven't heard it before (maybe!), so you open the door of communication to these older persons. Listen, show interest, and don't forget to praise them wherever the account shows good attitudes or actions on their part.

I often read a few verses from the Bible that are reassuring and comforting, and pray briefly with these friends, mentioning their personal needs specifically. When there's an appropriate opening, I find they enjoy talking about the future as well as the past — about heaven, reunion with loved ones, and the wonderful experience of seeing the Lord Jesus face to face.

But I believe that often what these older people need most is affection. The family they live with loves them and takes good care of them, but the wells of expressed affection sometimes seem to have dried up. So tell them you love them, that you remember them in your prayers, and that you miss them when they're away.

One of my little old ladies once said to me, "You're the only person who ever puts her arms around me any more, or gives me a kiss." So give yourself away — warmly, generously, and with enthusiasm — to some aging person who needs you. Do it for Christ's sake as well as for theirs.

The Lord has already given me a little old lady to love in the new neighborhood to which we have recently moved. She lives in an apartment just across the street from us. She's vivacious, cute, genuine, and loves the Lord Jesus. I look forward to my visits with her.

Give someone a shower, a surprise party, or a housewarming. Give a coffee for a new woman in the church. We all plan special occasions to honor our close friends, but there is an extra fillip of joy in doing something for someone others may have overlooked, or who doesn't have close friends locally who would do these loving things for him.

Folks usually attend the funerals of special friends or prominent people in our churches, but do you ever decide whether or not you will go to a funeral on the basis of how few others may be there? Put yourself in the place of the bereaved when hardly anyone comes to the funeral. Your presence among few may mean much more than where you would hardly have been missed among many.

When our daughter was still of an age that made long trips difficult, a woman in our church came to the house, just before a departure, with a box full of small packages for our Lorraine to open at stated intervals on the long pilgrimage we faced. It quite transformed the trip, and on the strength of that experience I have made similar travel kits for the children of friends. The gifts can be quite trivial but should aim to occupy the small fry en route.

Certainly not least in this list of practical helps is prayer. This too is love in action. And when God leads you to pray the prayer of faith for another's need, get ready for an answer.

If Christians were more honest and open with each other they could pray more specifically for practical needs. If we don't admit our needs, we cheat ourselves out of effective prayer help.

Don't promise to pray for someone unless you intend to do it. And when you *do* agree to pray, get your friend to promise to let you know when your prayer has been answered.

Many times we ought to do *more* than pray for a need — we should offer other practical help (a meal, transportation to the doctor, or even a cash gift). But sometimes when we busy ourselves with this kind of help we fail also to pray definitely and faithfully about the situation.

Paul wrote to his friends, "Pray always for all God's people. *And pray also for me.*"[31] It's easy to pray as our five-year old used to: " . . . and bless all the people in the world." But every Christian needs friends who will pray for his needs in particular.

A list of God's varied gifts to the Church includes "those who are given the power . . . to help others."[32] Some Christians are as specially endowed by God to help others as some are to preach or teach. They deserve as much honor as those who carry on a more conspicuous ministry. Paul wrote about three helpers who had come to him, "They have cheered me up just as they cheered you up. Such men as these deserve notice."[33]

Hospitality

One of the most practical expressions of love among the early Christians was their sharing meals and homes with each other. "Above everything," wrote the Apostle Peter, "love one another earnestly. . . . Open your homes to each other without complaining."[34]

Jesus added, as He sent His disciples out into remote areas where they would be dependent upon the hospitality of sympathetic listeners, "Whoever welcomes you, welcomes me. . . . Whoever welcomes God's messenger because he is God's messenger will share in his reward."[35] And at the time of judgment we hear Him say to His children who have fed the hungry and given them drink, who have invited destitute strangers into their homes and clothed them, who have cared for the sick and visited prisoners, "I tell you, indeed, whenever you did this for one of the least important of these brothers of mine, you did it for me."[36]

In the first century, travel was difficult and hotel accommodations often nonexistent. Christian hospitality was a necessity. Today it is perhaps more optional, but it still meets urgent needs among Christians — the need for acceptance, fellowship, and love.

Entertaining friends in one's home involves time and work and some expense, but when it is done to meet the needs of fellow Christians rather than for social advantage, it can be delightful and rewarding.

I once asked a hostess, who produced beautiful tables and delicious food with seeming ease, the secret of her poise. She answered quietly, "It's all in your motives." It made me examine mine. Are we trying to impress people or enjoy them and minister to their needs? Are we doing it for Christ's sake or our own?

Jesus had some plain things to say about whom we entertain. "When you give a lunch or a dinner, do not invite your friends . . . or your relatives, or your rich neighbors — for they will invite you back and in this way you will be paid for what you did. When you give a feast, invite the poor, the crippled, the lame, and the blind, and you will be blessed; for they are not able to pay you back. You will be paid by God when the good people are raised from death."[37]

This is hospitality offered not in order to get a return invitation but to meet personal need. This doesn't mean you should never entertain your relatives and friends. It does mean that the focus of your hospitality should be giving, not getting. I'm sure that is what my friend meant when she said that entertaining without tension depends on right motives. If we give our time and effort (and pay the bill) because we love and are concerned about our guests, then we can do it, as Peter said, "without complaining."

Who are some of the people who can't repay your kindness? Young people who still live with their parents or who are away from home at school. (How we have loved sharing our home with college students!) People who live in facilities that are inadequate in some way for entertaining. Folks who are short of money. A single or widowed man (or one whose wife is temporarily away), or a family where the mother is hospitalized, or a family that is in the process of moving.

The early Christians were charged especially to provide hospitality for Christian workers. "Please help them to continue their trip in a way that will please God. For they set out on their trip in the service of Christ. . . . We Christians, then, must help these men so that we may share in their work for the truth."[38]

The Christian workers you know may not be traveling, but they still need the love and encouragement you can give. Inviting them into your home lets them know that you care about them and support their ministry. Don't be too sure that your pastor's family have more invitations than they can handle. You might be surprised to know how few and far between their invitations sometimes are.

I once emceed a panel discussion of the personal needs of missionaries. The panel was made up of missionaries, and they surprised their audience by reporting that they would like to be invited more often into the homes of church members, adding that they usually were flooded with invitations at the time they could least comfortably accept them — just before furlough-end when they were packing to return to the field.

An invitation to dinner can be a warmhearted thank-you for the faithful service of a Sunday school teacher or youth leader. Have you ever invited the superintendent of your Sunday school to dinner because you appreciated his service to your family and church? What about the church custodian, the choir director, or the organist?

I remember one occasion while my husband was superintending our Sunday school when our hostess invited us, the pastors, and the church staff to her home after a Sunday evening service. She and her husband wanted in this way to show their respect and support of these leaders. It did us all good.

New people in a church have a special need to feel accepted and to get acquainted. If you invite some old-timers along with them, be sure that they are introduced to each one in a way that will help the newcomers remember names and faces.

Get them to tell about themselves, their background, where they have lived, what work they have done, and what family they have. You can usually add a bit of spice and interest by asking how this husband and wife met, and also how they came to attend your church.

"Remember to welcome strangers in your homes. There were some who did it and welcomed angels without knowing it."[39] I know of a young man who fell into conversation with a hippie at O'Hare Airport, took him home with him, and won him to Christ.

Widows who qualified for relief funds in the New Testament Church, among other things had to "have a reputation for good deeds: be a woman who brought up her children well, received strangers in her home, washed the feet of God's people, helped those in trouble, and gave herself to all kinds of good works."[40]

One of the qualifications for a man who was to be a leader in the church was, "He must welcome strangers in his home"[41] and "be hospitable."[42] This is important to God and profitable for His Church.

How Many?

My husband and I have disagreed for some time about

whether to invite more or fewer guests at one time. Our table seats eight, and because of all the preparation involved, it seems more efficient to entertain three other couples, but my husband always insists that communication is better with only one, or maybe two, other couples.

I remember one Sunday night when we had invited two couples in after church — one of them rather new. At the last minute, the other guests couldn't come, so we spent the evening with our new friends. They shared with us (as they never would have done if the others had been present) some problems and griefs related to their children. We were able not only to talk about their problems together but to pray about them.

Little by little, I have come to share my husband's feeling that we get to know people much better when a third couple isn't present. This is not a hard-and-fast rule, but we now usually follow it. For people who entertain a great deal and are invited out constantly, however, it may be impractical to invite so few at a time.

Let me suggest at this point that you think and pray carefully about just how much social life you really want.

I have one friend who entertains the deaconesses for lunch on Wednesday, has eight for dinner on Friday, and ten for an evening buffet on Sunday. How much additional time she and her husband spend being entertained in other people's homes I don't know, but I do know that I simply couldn't take on that amount of social activity.

We sometimes invite friends in after church on Sunday nights, or for dinner. But I remember the day when, after one of the few luncheons I ever produced for a group of women, I decided that (with a few exceptions) I would stick to dinners and Sunday nights. I simply would not enter the league of women's luncheons. I had too many other interests and would have had to sacrifice things I'd rather do.

So decide how you will use your time — how much of a social whirl you can afford — and then do gladly what you do do for the people you invite into your home.

The most important thing I have to say about entertaining is my conviction that we Christians would do better if we invited folks into our homes more often and did things more simply.

In the midwest community from which we have recently moved, Sunday night entertaining after church was a glamorous affair. When I was the hostess, I worked part of Saturday and most of Sunday afternoon getting the food and table ready, along with some extra housekeeping flourishes. And then I didn't produce the kind of elegant and elaborate affairs we enjoyed in some other homes.

One woman in our church told me that she so wished she could invite folks in for just doughnuts and coffee. Another said she never entertained because she didn't have a silver coffee service. I assured her I had never had one but that I entertained happily with what I had.

Most of our invitations out were as part of a larger group, and we enjoyed them. But with eight or ten persons present, or even more, we usually got to talk with only two or three individuals, and those conversations were largely superficial chit-chat. It is almost impossible to carry on a general and meaningful conversation with so large a group participating.

Often I would find myself geographically marooned with a cluster of women (whose conversation was not exactly absorbing) while with one ear I tried to listen in on a more rewarding discussion over on the men's side of the room and wishing all of us could have been in on it.

I am delighted that entertaining in our new southwest world seems to be less elaborate and more casual and relaxed. I remember the first Sunday night a couple took us home after church, impromptu fashion. They had a beautiful home, but sat us down to their table and proceeded to serve chocolate cake and coffee. It didn't pretend to be a buffet or a "meal," but it was good, and the conversation was delightful.

Following their example, we entertained couples from our Sunday school class on a regular basis, serving only dessert and coffee. Because it was easy, I could do it more often.

You may be able to entertain on a more elaborate scale, but in doing so you may discourage other Christians from opening their homes to friends because they can't keep up with your style.

I'm convinced that Christian fellowship in the home would be improved if we gave less thought to the food and more to the conversation. When we have several guests, my husband and I — aiming for group conversation — make an effort to prevent the men from all sitting together after we leave the table, and this usually results in more general conversation. Sometimes we let our guests know ahead of time that we plan a discussion of some announced subject of common interest. This insures discussion by the entire group. Pick a topic according to the age and interests of your folks. You could discuss:

How to get along with neighbors
Why your Sunday school isn't growing
How to survive living with teen-agers
How being a Christian helps or complicates things on your job
Preparations people should make for their families in case of sudden death (Get a lawyer to give some practical advice)
How to improve your personal or family devotions
How to choose books to read, or How to improve your church library
What to do at home about pollution

Or you might suggest that your guests read a specified article in some magazine available to most of them, perhaps the *Readers Digest.*

I remember one evening when we discussed an article about becoming the best person you can be. We were delighted to observe that one friend who was outstandingly successful in business affairs was equally able and articulate as a thinker in areas of personality, psychology, and human relationships. Our subject was secular, but we enjoyed relating it to our Christian perspective.

We recently participated in two stimulating discussions. One, what our class of couples in their thirties could undertake as a project of joint action to put into practice what they were learning in their Bible study sessions. The other, a discussion of what kind of pastor we wanted for our church, to fill the place of the one who had recently resigned. Instead of breaking up into an assortment of miniscule conversations, the group listened and participated as a whole, and the exchange was interesting and profitable.

Too often there is little meeting of minds, and little effort to understand others or make ourselves known to them. A host who is aware of this tendency can do a good deal to direct conversation (even if it isn't formally planned), especially in getting guests to tell about themselves.

For example, ask each guest to tell something about his job — what he actually does. When our Sunday school class gave us a housewarming on our wedding anniversary, we suggested that each couple tell where they were married and where they spent their honeymoon. It was fun and gave all a chance to share themselves with the others.

Someone has said that people play games when they come together because this enables them to escape being alone and yet avoids the responsibility of making conversation. I enjoy games and certainly there is a legitimate place for them, but good conversational interaction is even better.

A Christian who is not concerned about impressing people himself can do much to open the way for others to share themselves with the group. Casually ask a newcomer to tell about his background; a fall group to report on their vacations; holiday guests to reminisce on what they remember about their childhood Christmases; someone who has a new job to describe what he is doing.

Or, give grandparents (if your guests are older people) three to five minutes each (you'll need a stop watch!) to tell about their grandchildren. Ask one of your guests to express an opinion on some open-ended subject such as how a church can be truly friendly.

If you get into a controversial area and feelings intensify, remind folks that everyone has a right to his opinion whether others agree with him or not.

One of the secrets of good conversation is to be genuinely interested in what other people say. Ask a question based on what someone has said, and encourage others to express their opinions or experience in the area.

As a mother, let me add one more suggestion. When guests bring a child to your home — perhaps for dinner — recognize him as a person. Too often, adults simply act as though the child were not there. Bring him into the conversation now and then. Ask him a question and show an interest in his world as well as in his parents. It is nothing short of rude to act as though a youngster were as inanimate as the chair he sits on.

The wonderful thing about giving yourself away — giving yourself to people for Christ's sake — is that this kind of giving enriches rather than depletes you. You don't do it in order to get friends, but when you set self aside to serve the needs of others you are a friend in the truest sense, whether or not people recognize it.

As we shall see in the next chapter, self-giving is the best cure for loneliness; it meets your own needs while it ministers to others'. "Your own soul is nourished when you are kind; it is destroyed when you are cruel."[43]

Dr. George S. Stevenson, writing about how to deal with your tensions, advises, "If you worry about yourself all the time, try doing something for somebody else. This will take the steam out of your worries and, even better, give you a warm feeling of having done well."[44]

"The world is composed of takers and givers. The takers may eat better, but the givers sleep better."[45]

8

HELP! I'M *OUT!*

Stanley is sixteen. He is tall and skinny, somewhat homely, shy and slow-spoken. Even though he is healthy enough, he can't participate in sports because years ago rheumatic fever left him with heart damage. He has a flair for science courses and plays phenomenal chess.

His mother is a Christian but his father, a businessman with a less-than-savory reputation, never comes to services, so his family are not socially settled in the church Stanley attends. Currently this young Christian doesn't have any personal friends among the young people and feels so rejected and miserable that he doesn't know whether or not to keep coming.

Stanley also doesn't know that he will put on twenty-five pounds before he finishes college and will afterwards become a respected research chemist.

Don and Shelley Mason attend another church, but have failed to find friends there. Neither of them is shy or unable to carry on a conversation. In fact they "carry" all of it.

When the Masons were new in the church, the pastor and his wife invited them, with another new couple, to the parsonage. At the evening's end, the pastor had really gotten to know the Masons. They had traveled a great deal and could tell the most interesting experiences — one after another — to their spellbound audience. Their vivacity and enthusiasm filled the room, but after a while one became aware that nobody else was having a chance to contribute anything more than an occasional grunt or comment related to the Masons' recital.

The pastor and his wife didn't get acquainted with the other couple at all that night.

Concerned as to just how the Masons were being received by other members of the congregation, the pastor's wife asked one of the church women if she thought they were getting acquainted and feeling at home.

"I don't know," was the uncertain response. "We had them in with another couple after church one Sunday night and the other couple might just as well not have been there!"

How this pastor's wife longed to help the Masons realize that in their eagerness to "go over" with new acquaintances they were defeating their own end by monopolizing the conversation! (The Masons are thinking of trying a "more friendly" church.)

Are you a Stanley, a Don, or a Shelley? If you are left out because, like Stanley, you feel inferior in some way, or because, like the Masons, you feel other people don't respond to you as they should, you're not alone. Your fellow sufferers hide their inner wistfulness or bitterness behind a brave façade of "we're okay," or "we-don't-need-anyone." But underneath, they're dissatisfied either with themselves or with other people's reaction to them. They need help but probably won't ask for it.

If you have never experienced loneliness — the pain of feeling unwanted and excluded — don't think that such feelings in others are unreal or unimportant, or that they have nothing to do with *you*. They do, and you can't ignore them if you want to fulfil Christ's command that His people love one another. You have a personal responsibility to help meet the acute need that exists in the lives of many Christians, young and old.

A few sturdy souls care little or nothing about what people think of them. They are so rugged and thick-skinned that they can meet indifference or even rejection without pain. But most people cannot.

This chapter speaks to all of you who lack social acceptance in your local church — those who are less sensitive and those who find the experience painful. We will touch on some areas already mentioned in earlier chapters, but will focus here on your personal problem.

Self-Poisoning

Because your problem revolves around yourself, it's easy for you to become self-centered. Lepp says that egocentricity is not an excess of self-love but a lack of it — a way of compensating for feeling inferior or inadequate. You become preoccupied with yourself because others don't pay attention to you.

A visiting psychologist observed in the patients in a sanatorium "a lonely preoccupation with the self that had poisoned the mind." This was why they were there.

Someone has defined an unlovely package as a person all wrapped up in himself and usually fit to be tied.

When people don't like you, you either blame them or dislike yourself. Both attitudes may be factors in your failure to find friends, but the place to begin is always with yourself. Ask God to show you where you need to be changed, and then count on Him to make such changes possible in you. *You* must want to change and *you* must do it, but *God* will give you the power to become a renewed person.

Ask, "Create in me a clean heart, O God; and renew a right spirit within me."[1] He can open doors to personal development that you couldn't open without Him.

If you have actually come into a personal relationship with Jesus Christ, you should have, in addition to God's supernatural power, a new view of self and of life. You don't lose your personal identity and distinctiveness when you become a Christian, but self and its strong demands are brought under the control of Christ.

The New Testament calls this experience a death and a resurrection. "I have been put to death with Christ on his cross," says Paul, "so that it is no longer I who live, but it is Christ who lives in me."[2] "You have died. . . . You have been raised to life with Christ . . . and your life is hidden with Christ in God. Your real life is Christ."[3] Living the Christian life is far more than merely trying to act like Christ. It is letting

Christ live His own wonderful life in you.

No wonder Paul links important conclusions to this truth: "Why, then, do you live as though you belonged to this world? . . . Set your hearts, then, on the things that are in heaven . . . not on things here on earth."[4]

A Christian's goals and attitudes are radically changed. He can know deliverance from his own selfish demands as he allows Christ to live His resurrection life in and through him. This is the new self, committed to and delighting in doing the will of God.

Put the right label on a passion for popularity: it's the old self making its demands. There's nothing sinful about needing and wanting acceptance and friends. Don't be ashamed to admit that you do. But if you become preoccupied with that desire for attention, if you allow it to poison your whole personality and life perspective, you need to go back to the Cross. There, if you are a Christian, you said to God with Christ, "Not my will . . . but your will be done."[5] There self came under the all-wise, all-loving control of God Almighty. Renew this commitment often!

Understanding this Christian view of self is the very groundwork of right relations between a Christian and every other person his life touches. As you turn yourself over to God, you can accept yourself and your situation. You not only belong to Him but He is at work in you, changing you to be His person and to experience His good plan for you.

Once this truth becomes real to you, you have a new view of all your human relationships, and can commit your need of friends to Him. Your person and your life are in His hands, not other people's.

God will help you to evaluate your strengths and weaknesses and to recognize your limitations without bitterness. He knows you completely and loves and plans for you. So accept yourself as He accepts you — aware of what can't be changed but also aware that wonderful development *is possible* to you.

Feel — Think

Years ago I was arrested by this pert phrase: "Don't just

feel, *think!"* When we are overwhelmed by emotions — disappointment, hurt, resentment, anger, or even pleasure — it's good to set aside strong feelings long enough to think through the situation that is producing them.

Try it when you feel inferior or inadequate, lonely or rejected. Think about what you are and why others react to you as they do. Take note of the many Christians who are fine people but aren't numbered among the *Ins*. Think about how God sees your situation and what He can do about it. Thinking carefully and praying about the whole business — talking it over with the Lord — will relieve those feelings that are smothering you.

Many people of distinction were not and are not popular with their peers, especially in their home communities. Among them were Joseph, Moses, Stephen, and Jesus.

I know a woman of little background and few cultural advantages who showed extraordinary talent in her mature years. She is beautiful, has enough personality for ten people, and is both genuine and charming. Yet she once said to me, "Whenever I meet new people I'm saying inwardly, 'Please like me!' "

Lonely people aren't necessarily inferior; sometimes they are gifted and superior.

Me to Blame?

Be sure you are your *best* self. Check the tests in Chapter 4. Think especially about the characteristics that often repel people. Here are a few that have to do with your physical exterior.

Personal cleanliness is important. I have known people who were well educated and successful, career-wise, who had a terribly strong body odor that one could recognize six feet away, or that struck you as they stepped into a room.

I wondered if one man ever took a bath. One day his wife remarked that he was taking a shower, yet when he came into the room the left-over odor on his clothes overwhelmed any benefits of the ablutions.

I know one father who took the bull by the horns and told his daughter as lovingly as possible that she had chronic body odor. She has showered religiously every morning for years since then, and never offends.

Bad breath is another problem that also simply may be a physical trait, not the result of carelessness. The one who has it may not know it, but if you ask your best friend, he may tell you the truth. And any human being with eyes and ears knows the products that deal with this problem!

Are you overweight? Rotund young people often suffer from lack of friends and dates, and sometimes the more they worry, the more they eat, and the more they eat, the more they weigh! A vicious circle, but one from which there is an exit wide enough to let you out! *Think!* Which do you want most — more pizzas, banana splits, and candy bars, or a boyfriend or girl friend, or other friends who aren't embarrassed to be seen with you?

Pehaps you're not only plain looking but downright homely, or even repulsive looking — deformed or disfigured in some way. This is something you probably can't change but must accept if you have hope that others will accept you. Actually, it may be easier for them to accept you than for you to accept yourself, but with God's help you can do it. More than that, He can give you another sort of beauty that is real and rare, and that others will value.

> Some folks in looks take so much pride
> They don't think much of what's inside.
> Well, as for me, I know my face
> Can ne'er be made a thing of grace.
> And so I rather think I'll see
> How I can fix th' inside o' me
> So folks'll say, "He looks like sin,
> But ain't he beautiful within!"[6]

I think of two striking examples of this beauty. One was the speaker at a librarians' banquet in Philadelphia. His face was so scarred or disfigured I thought I would never be able to look at him during his address. But his mind and his words were so rich and stimulating that nothing else registered during those magic moments.

The other is a woman who has a deforming curvature of the spine, yet has become a fine Christian educator and editor —

a confident, shining person.

"The chief problem, often the only obstacle to the birth of friendship," says Lepp, "exists in the subject himself who complains of not having any friends."[7] Is what you really need more attention from people or improved character, personality, and attitudes? Never say, "This is how I am. I can't change." *Expect* to change, grow, develop, and mature as a result of God's working in you.

Be open to constructive criticism. "Anyone willing to be corrected is on the pathway to life."[8]

"Don't refuse to accept criticism; get all the help you can."[9]

"If you profit from constructive criticism you will be elected to the wise man's hall of fame. But to reject criticism is to harm yourself and your own best interests."[10]

A little neighbor boy rang my doorbell one day after school. "Denny and Paul won't play with me," he complained. "Are you nice to play with?" I asked quietly. He gave me a long, surprised look, turned on his heel, and walked away silently.

People react to social failure in different ways. Tournier, in *Escape from Loneliness,* says that the socially unintegrated fall into an exaggerated self-analysis and into faultfinding.[11]

When we feel that others have found us lacking, we immediately begin to find fault with them. It becomes a sort of self-justification. "You don't like me, but I see faults in you, too, so don't think you're so much better than I am, even if you do have more friends!"

We may not put it into so many words, but this is the way we comfort ourselves. And whether we are forever turned inward in self-examination or outward in quest of flaws in others, we are inevitably cutting ourselves off from the very people we so badly need.

Accept other Christians as they are, and accept even the quality of their response to you. Be open to them without feelings of resentment, and see what it will do to your own spirit and to their response to you!

I'll Show Them!

Some Christians who have had to come face to face with

their unpopularity become so resentful and bitter (not to say "sour") that it seems almost impossible to get through to them.

One Sunday school class member said of another, who is unusually arbitrary in his views, critical of other Christians, and thoroughly gruff and defensive about his own bristly self, "He just sits back there in his corner and dares you to love him." We were pleased to discover that actually this man was approachable and open to friendship, but his whole manner would discourage most people.

Are you open to people — or closed?

Resentment may lead to retaliation — finding subtle ways of getting even with those who have bypassed you. You may look for an opportunity to show them your ill will or you may talk about them in an effort to degrade them in the eyes of others.

When the people of a Samaritan village refused to receive Jesus, His disciples reacted by asking, "Lord, do you want us to call fire down from heaven and destroy them?"[12] Jesus rebuked them.

A sense of personal insecurity may lay you open to hurts that are largely imagined. Someone has labeled this attitude, "Not enough personal vigor of spirit to *shed* slight or unintentional rebuffs." You file away, for future reference, the remark or act or even just a look, and bring it out often to refresh your memory.

Or you may enjoy going to the offender and being "honest" by letting him know how this bit of trivia hurt you, and giving him an opportunity to apologize! This won't so much show up his fault as reveal your own small dimensions. There is a right time to deal with more serious wounds, but don't imagine that it comes often.

Make it a practice to put the best possible construction on what people say and do. Don't be thin-skinned and hypersensitive. Some socially insecure folks are impossible to please. If you don't pay them attention they resent it, but the moment you *do* pay them attention they suspect you of condescension, insincerity, and wrong motives, and subtly let you know that they see through you and don't appreciate your effort.

We have found this to be true in some of our attempts to be friendly to our black brothers in Christ. They seem to resent normal friendliness, and accuse us either of condescension and insincerity or of snobbishness. One of them, reporting on the friendliness of Christians in a church where he had visited, announced with finality, "They all shook hands and smiled at us, but we knew they didn't really mean it."

With a few happy exceptions in our experience, some of us are close to giving up trying to please these fellow Christians we so much want to include in simple, sincere loving. But we must remember how hard it is for them, having been socially rejected for generations — especially by the Christian Church — to trust our offer of friendship today. And we had better examine with thoroughness the quality of the friendship we offer!

Some who long for personal acceptance (and some who find it) travel the road of conformity. Instead of being themselves, they try hard to be like the people they hope will accept them.

Burkhart says of an individual who is so strongly committed to the crowd, "As a person he has no meaning. . . . no real identity. If he comes to the group totally on its own terms, then membership is a denial of his own individuality. He does not think, he paraphrases; he has no convictions, he chants the group thoughts; he is a slave, for he submits to the group stereotypes."[13]

This can be pathetically true even in a Christian group. I don't know which is more pathetic — a desperate conformist, or an *In* group that rejects a sincere Christian simply because he is different in matters of personal appearance, current local church issues, minor biblical interpretation, or questionable practices.

Christians who play God — judging other Christians in these areas and equating their own personal tastes, interpretations, or opinions with the absolute will of God — will have to answer to Him for their unloving vindictiveness.

Let me say again: whatever else you do, don't relieve your feeling of being rejected by rejecting someone else. When you've been made to feel inferior, don't boost your ego by showing some other person that you consider him inferior to *you*.

"When a poor man oppresses those even poorer, he is like

an unexpected flood sweeping away their last hope."[14] Sometimes those who are low on the totem pole may actually be much more arrogant than those near the top.

"Do you, my friend, pass judgment on others? You have no excuse at all, whoever you are. For when you judge others, but do the same things that they do, you condemn yourself."[15]

Sometimes a socially insecure person — a young person especially — may react to his problem by making foolish and even wild bids for attention. "A man may ruin his chances by his own foolishness and then blame it on the Lord!"[16] He may resort to outlandish gestures, boisterous talk, or bits of gossip made sensational by exaggeration or actual untruth.

I remember a girl in a youth group I sponsored years ago who just didn't make it with the *In* group but who managed almost habitually to gather around her a crowd of listeners she would electrify with her startling and sometimes malicious conversation. She was fun to listen to but not the kind of person her peers wanted for a personal friend.

I remember too my own performance as a young teen-ager whose older sister was more popular with the boys. After a swimming party, I swatted one of her admirers with a rolled-up bathing suit, endearing myself to him as the donor of a black eye.

People who resort to these methods of getting attention are unconsciously admitting their own social insecurity, and this usually defeats their attempt to win acceptance. Most of us don't want conspicuous people as personal friends. So never say or do things that don't rightly represent the real you, simply because, at the moment, you think they might appear impressive. You will probably regret it later.

Other social rejects simply give up, withdraw from people, and avoid contacts that might expose them to rejection again. An artist describing his unhappy life wrote, "It seems to me that the same pattern runs through my whole life, my painting, my relationships with people, everything. I'm afraid to open up, commit myself. I'm beginning to think that it's because I felt so rejected as a child. My trouble is that I'm terrified of being rejected again."[17]

Or, if you don't withdraw from social contacts, you may put on the act of pretending that you have no need for friends.

I remember one couple who attended a fairly large group to which we belonged. I didn't know their names, but when I would resolve to engage them in conversation at the close of a session I would be discouraged by the way they made their exodus — eyes straight to the front, and stepping forward with such intensity that you felt they must be rushing to the choir loft to sing a duet at the next service, or keeping an appointment with the President of the United States. The next chapter will tell how we finally got acquainted.

There are other attitudes you may not recognize in yourself that may be contributing to your unpopularity. Take a look with me at a few not-so-popular people I have met.

Sally — often encountered in the supermarket — would sidle up to me, her opening remark spoken in a half-whisper behind the back of her hand: "Didja hear . . . ?"

Scott is aggressive, stepping into leadership openings almost before anyone can decide whether or not he is qualified. He does his job, but is so arbitrary and domineering that those who try to work with him wince. He doesn't mean to be overbearing, but he is, and invariably those who work with him are offended or simply drift out of the project.

Pam is popular, but though she wins an election easily, her peers are disappointed in her because she doesn't meet her responsibilities, and everyone feels she has let them down.

Kay and her husband were invited to a small potluck dinner. Kay was to bring the meat. Perennially late, she arrived one whole hour late this time, and the meat she brought was uncooked! (This is a true incident.)

Some couples we have known and entertained *never* invite friends to their homes. They simply state, "We never entertain." Having friends, however, isn't a one-way street. It's the shared delight of receiving and giving.

One of the most incredible situations I have heard of is a couple who frankly declare, "We never invite to our home anyone who earns more than $7,000 a year." How do they know the incomes of the folks in their church? And is that economic level an insurmountable barrier to Christian fellowship? If it ever is, it's a poor commentary on relationships among God's people.

I have heard of a number of folks who complained that they weren't accepted in their church who, nevertheless, seldom invited back the folks who had entertained them. One such couple, who had been in our church for more than a year, remarked to me that people had paid them a lot of attention when they first came but had seemed indifferent in recent months.

"Why, you're not newcomers anymore," I suggested. "By now you should be busy making other folks feel at home, not still looking for attention."

The Mouth

Before going on to some positive suggestions about how to handle your social insecurity, let's think about the Masons' problem which was mentioned at the beginning of this chapter.

They didn't bore people by *what* they said. Their talk was interesting, but it all turned in on themselves instead of reaching out to bring others into the conversation. They talked too much, leaving the less articulate to sit like lumps and listen. And even a person who isn't conversationally gifted likes to contribute at least once in a while!

Perhaps you make the mistake of feeling uncomfortable when you're not talking — as though you were somehow socially inadequate if you couldn't keep chattering. Remember that being able to say nothing and still feel comfortable is a mark of poise — unless, of course, you fail ever to say anything!

I know a number of people who are so quick to jump into an opening in a conversation that it's almost impossible to beat them to it, and others usually give up, sit back, and try to figure out why this garrulous individual is such a compulsive talker. Perhaps I'm particularly aware of this fault because I like to talk and have had to discipline myself in this area.

Compulsive talkers often don't wait for an opening in the conversation. They *can't* wait. So they interrupt you near (hopefully!) the end of a sentence. With a few such chronic interrupters, I have on occasion come to the point of asking as sweetly as possible, "Would you mind if I finished what I was saying?" Interrupting another person is never anything but rude, and you can get yourself thoroughly disliked if you make a practice of it.

Another "problem of the mouth" that has troubled us in meeting other couples has been a situation in which either the husband or the wife does *all* the talking for the pair. The partner is never able to get a toehold in the conversation. In one case the husband is slow- and low-spoken but completely charming — when his wife is not present and he has a chance. But when she's there, she does *all* the talking. Even if you address your question to him by name, she pops right in with the answer. She doesn't so much detract from him personally, as exhibit her own insensitivity, poor taste, and bad manners.

Another couple does it in reverse. She is gentle-voiced but witty and delightful. He is quite colorless by comparison, but drones on endlessly over boring details of his past without ever giving her a chance to speak up. If you're half a couple, listen to yourself, and while you're at it maybe you should listen to your better (?) half!

Giggling is another conversational blemish that is habitual with some people. It's a sure sign of being nervous and ill at ease, of needing to fill in every fractional moment with a sound if you can't produce a word, or of unconsciously trying to make what you say seem nonchalant, breezy, and happy.

I can sound forth eloquently on this subject because at the ripe age of thirty-nine I sat on the proverbial sofa with a man I had known for only a few weeks. Being "courted" at this advanced age was an experience, and I must have shown my sense of tension.

Without warning he said quietly to me, "Stop giggling." I would have blacked his eye on the spot if, by counting to ten first, I hadn't had time to realize that I had been ornamenting our communication with numerous titters. It was an awful moment, but it was a moment of truth, and I married him anyway!

Since then I have noticed that sound of unease often and repeatedly in others. One was a middle-aged missionary who stayed in our home overnight and who for no reason at all giggled the whole length of a flight of stairs as she bade us goodnight over her shoulder.

If you giggle, *listen* to yourself! If you think you don't giggle, listen anyway. You may make a discovery!

Another kind of talk that may not win you friends is the cute, witty, smart retort. People are impressed by your ability to come up instantly with something so clever and apropos. Such wits are fun to listen to, but their remarks are sometimes cutting, even devastating. This kind of talk may make you popular with a certain sophisticated crowd, but most people will feel incapable of verbal exchange that matches your wit, and will prefer friends who are perhaps less clever but more polite, sincere, kind, and merciful.

Some people are painful conversationalists because they tell everything in such boring detail. They struggle over the day of the week on which their third child came down with the measles twelve years ago, or haggle with their spouse over how much they paid for a motel room in Miami the winter before last. They describe in detail each hour of each of the ten days they just spent in the hospital, without ever suspecting that their audience would appreciate a much briefer account.

Some folks, on the contrary, have nothing to say on their own, and never even comment on or ask an interested question about what other people contribute.

I remember Lynne — a highly intelligent and creative college girl who came to our home often but who said so little that carrying on a conversation with her became a great effort on our part. She prided herself on saying nothing except when she "had something to say."

I remember, on different occasions, showing her my white amaryllis in full bloom, a poem our daughter had written, and a new set of dining room furniture. I really didn't want her to rave, but when there was no response but silence I would resolve each time to restrain my enthusiasms and never try to share them with her again.

But one summer she became a local playground supervisor and shared an apartment with other girls involved in the project. She rarely initiated conversation with them or helped to keep one going, and the girls finally told her off.

They convinced her that she too had a responsibility to make being together a pleasant and comfortable experience. And Lynne was "big" enough to accept the criticism and to share it with me.

It was a delight to see the change that took place in her. As a committed Christian, she came to see that giving herself to others, and responding to them, is an important part of good personal relationships. She became a much more enjoyable visitor.

A hostess appreciates a guest who both contributes to the conversation and responds with interest to what others have to say. Instead of frantically trying to think of something to "tell" next, listen with concentration to what others say and react with interest and questions.

We recently shared an evening with a doctor-friend, and I noticed several times how he responded thoughtfully to something that had been said, with the comment, "That's very interesting." It made you feel that what you had said had been well received and, rather than bringing the subject to an end, led into further discussion of it.

You can develop these conversational graces if you will, and it will help make you a welcome addition to any group.

"The words of a wise man's mouth are gracious, but the lips of a fool will swallow up himself."[18]

"A fool gets into constant fights. His mouth is his undoing! His words endanger him."[19]

"Everyone enjoys giving good advice, and how wonderful it is to be able to say the right thing at the right time!"[20]

"Don't talk so much. You keep putting your foot in your mouth. Be sensible and turn off the flow."[21]

"A fool's voice is known by a multitude of words."[22]

"Let your speech always be gracious, seasoned with salt."[23]

"A word fitly spoken is like apples of gold in pictures of silver."[24]

Listen to yourself the next time you get together with friends. Are you interesting or boring? Interested in or indifferent to others? Kind or cutting? An asset or a handicap to good conversation?

Tackle Your Problem

Zacchaeus was frustrated because of his inability to make personal contact with someone who was out of his reach. He wanted access to Jesus, but the crowd was great and Zacchaeus was small — too short to make his way to this important Person.

But Zacchaeus didn't give up and wallow in self-pity. He didn't demand that others step aside, but he *did* find a place for himself — not a prime position, but one he wasn't too proud to use. He climbed a tree, and in that unlikely place he made contact with the One he wanted to know.[25]

You have a problem — an inability to make touch with people. Whatever your handicaps may be, don't indulge in self-pity nor demand that others make way for you. Size up your limitations and your problem and then do what you can to solve it.

To begin with, God is interested in your personal need. "The Holy Spirit . . . does not want you to be afraid of people, but to be wise and strong, and to love them and enjoy being with them."[26] Do you believe that? If you do, it will make a big difference in your attitude toward your problem and your attitude toward people.

If you realize you can't simply push your way into personal relationships with some folks you would like as friends, accept and treasure the friends you already have or others who are available to you.

It's healthy to accept gracefully the fact that you don't fit in, or aren't wanted or needed, in certain groups — to settle down and be comfortable and effective where you are. Live in the joy of what you have — your family, your church, your Lord — not in preoccupation with what you don't have.

Learn, as Paul did, to be satisfied and content. "How great is the joy I have in my life in the Lord! . . . I have learned to be satisfied with what I have. I know what it is to be in need, and what it is to have more than enough. I have learned this secret, so that anywhere, at any time, I am content, whether I am full or hungry, whether I have too much or too little. I have the strength to face all conditions by the power that Christ gives me."[27]

Perhaps what you need more than social acceptance is to learn to be content with what you already have.

Be realistic about yourself and your ambitions. Not all persons have equal capacity. Some are more modestly endowed and there will be no happiness for them until they recognize and accept this fact. If this is true of you, there's no reason why you should have a feeling of personal failure because you aren't as popular as someone else. You just *aren't* someone else.

Learning to accept yourself and your situation, and to enjoy the good things you have, will free you of resentment toward others and make it possible for you to meet them with genuine warmth and availability.

Respond to anyone who reaches out to you. Glory in a varied assortment of friends if you haven't (or if you have!) been assimilated into some cohesive group. Give yourself freely and with delight to all who touch your life. Actually this may be a far more rewarding social setup than being part of some select clique.

So, even though you hope for more friends, *don't try so hard. Don't care so much!* Relax!

You have accepted yourself and your situation. "You should have a dignified pride in being you. . . . You can never be anyone else . . . except a phony self. The struggle to be someone else will always fail. . . . Hoping to be admired is evidence of present dissatisfaction with yourself. Want to make an impression? Don't try! Pretense and artificiality never lead to happiness!"[28]

What other people think of you, or how popular you are, are really not of first importance. Don't be like the man who "drove himself and others unmercifully in his strenuous struggle for recognition."[29] Caring too much whether people like you or not can actually shut you off from friendship as well as give you ulcers.

"The tragedy is that the very ones who most desire to be loved are the ones who create a vacuum around them. . . . It is very difficult to show love to these hungry hearts. Their very desire creates the barrier to any affective relationship. So intensely do they want this heart-to-heart fellowship, and with so great fear of being deceived, that *they lose the ease and relaxation in which warm feelings are spontaneously set free.*[30] They elicit the very thing they expect because they lack the at-homeness and at-easeness that would give the acceptance they crave.

So commit your need to God, and then step out of the shadows of anxiety into the sunshine of confident trust.

"Don't worry about anything, but in all your prayers ask God for what you need, always asking Him with a thankful heart. And God's peace, which is far beyond human understanding, will keep your hearts and minds safe in Christ Jesus."[31]

Tell Somebody

If you feel emotionally pressured by lack of friends, share your concern with someone. I mentioned the woman whose husband sent her to me to unload this burden. There is psychological health in such sharing — and we each found a friend in the process!

I remember vividly one night when my husband admitted to me his feelings of inadequacy in relating to people. His confession was like a fresh breeze blowing across our communication, for it let me feel free to discuss with him what I had hidden before — my own desire for better rapport with individuals.

We both have delighted in the teaching ministries God has opened to us through the years — large classes and small — and the Lord has made them fruitful. But we felt a lack in our more personal relationships.

Should you be frank about your need with someone close to you? It may not only relieve you but may make way for the other person to share some need.

Your pastor or his wife may be the right one for you to confide in, or a Sunday school teacher who cares, or some warmhearted fellow Christian who has experienced his own heartaches and so has learned how to comfort and counsel others. But whomever you turn to, be straightforward and frank. Don't beat around the bush and only half state your need.

Don't look for a ready-made solution to your problem, either! Gather strength from knowing that the person you confide in cares about you, and make sure that he prays with you about your need before you leave.

Jacob Loewen tells of a Mrs. Woodrum, a widow of fifty-five, who jumped to her death one morning from her twelfth-floor apartment on Chicago's north side. On her orderly desk, Mrs. Woodrum left this note: "I can't stand one more day of this loneliness. No sound from my telephone. No mail in my box. No friends!"

Mrs. Jenkins, another widow, lived on the same floor of the same large apartment building. Later she told reporters, "I wish I had known she was lonely; I could have called on her. We could have been friends."

"Sociologists and psychologists of our Western culture," Loewen adds, "have noted the increase of social distance that is accompanying rapid urbanization. When men and women move to large urban centers, they leave behind them the familiarity of the rural areas. They often feel lost and alone in the impersonal city, but mask their insecurities with an aloof conventional smile, not realizing that the one at whom they flash this smile also wears a mask to cover the same insecurities."[32]

Don't refuse to ask for help because you're too proud to admit your need! Trust people — especially the Christians around you. And even if *they* fail you at some point, God never will.

George S. Stevenson, discussing "positive action you can take for yourself" in dealing with tensions, says, "Make yourself available. Many of us have the feeling that we are being 'left out,' slighted, neglected. Often we just imagine this. Instead of shrinking away and withdrawing, it is healthier — and more practical — to make overtures [to others] yourself. There is a middle ground between withdrawal and pushing. Try it."[33]

Years ago I was asked to write an article entitled "Meet

Your Mate on a Christian Campus" for an education issue of a Christian magazine. Armed with a pad, a pencil, and a list of thirteen questions, I invaded the campus of Wheaton College. In my conversations with men about dating, and the fact that some outstandingly attractive girls had few dates, one observation was made repeatedly: Men date girls who make themselves available.

This is not a tribute to boldness or aggressiveness in girls, but a window into the reluctance of men to date a girl the hard way. They shrink from approaching the object of their interest when she is always surrounded by one or more other females, and they don't like to go to a women's dorm or make their first approach over the house phone.

If a girl and a fellow are in the same class, and she leaves it alone and walks slowly enough, the fellow may catch up with her and make an easy start by discussing the class session. Or if she sometimes sits by herself in one of the lounges, he can easily make a beginning.

So, you students, don't avoid being alone. Don't be afraid of looking lost and lonely. Be person enough not always to need the crutch of someone else's presence in the hall, in the cafeteria, when you go for your mail. And don't seem to be in an everlasting hurry, plunging along so vigorously that no one dares to interrupt your progress. Walk slowly and enjoy every inch of the route you travel. Your relaxed ease will encourage friendliness.

What is true for a student is true for the rest of us. Are you like my husband, who prefers to sit near the door at a church service and go directly to the car when it's over? Sit nearer the front and go out deliberately, smiling at folks, making yourself available, but without being at all tensely concerned whether or not people come to you. Greet a stranger, show a genuine interest in people you know, be friendly to children and young people, and have a warm word for your pastor and his family.

You will not only learn to enjoy such friendly contacts, but will meet a real need in your church, for there are never enough such outgoing people in any congregation.

Even if you aren't talking to folks, linger a little as you go out, and take your time getting your wraps on and herding your children together. Many people who accuse Christians of being unfriendly hardly give them a chance.

Learn to initiate conversation. Ask some question related to the present situation like, "Did you get caught in that rain this morning?" Or, "How is that new granddaughter?" Or, "Have you heard from Tom since his unit went overseas?" Or, "I've missed you the last few Sundays, haven't I?"

Questions that can be answered by "yes" or "no" sometimes bring a conversation to an untimely end. Many folks you meet would be glad to talk with you but have trouble getting started. Make it easy for them.

Help to meet your own and others' need for warm social contacts by inviting missionaries on furlough to your home for a meal or refreshments. Entertain your pastor and your children's Sunday school teachers, and tell them how much you appreciate their ministry (even if it *isn't* perfect!). Invite to your home people who are new in the church, folks who may not be included in other groups, and students away from home. Don't sit around complaining that no one invites *you*. Furnish your own social life as you use your home to bless others.

Cure for Loneliness

Billy Graham advises lonely people, "Involve yourself in service to others. When some crisis strikes a community — such as a tornado, a blizzard, a flood — people   reach out, regardless of race or social distinction, to help each other. Yet many of the people we meet every day are experiencing inner floods, disasters, and tornadoes that can be more devastating than any physical storm."

Then he tells about a woman who wrote him of the boredom that came into her life when her children were grown and gone from home.

"In the past," he advised her, "your immediate family needed most of your time and strength. Now you can extend the range of your love. There are children in your neighborhood who need understanding and friendship. There are aged people near you who are starved for companionship, blind people who cannot even enjoy the television you find so boring. Why not get out and find the joy of helping others?"

Weeks later she wrote again: "I tried your prescription. It works! I have walked from night into day!"[34]

Ruth Millett, in a column on loneliness, says, "You should never complain that you're lonely unless during the past week you have —

"Done at least one kindness for someone who is worse off than you are.

"Telephoned at least three persons to find how *they* are getting along — not to tell them *your* troubles.

"Invited at least three persons to your home — even if the invitations were only casually asking a neighbor in for coffee or asking a friend to share a meal.

"Made plans to do at least one thing with someone else — even if it was just a shopping trip or taking someone for a drive."[35]

Get together with people regularly in the organized activities of your church or in Christian or secular organizations outside the church. This will broaden your horizons, fill up your calendar, and increase your personal contacts and opportunities to make new friends. Do it to fill your life and to serve God and others, but don't do it just to get friends!

Find a place in or out of your church where you can take responsibility — do a good service job. Work in the Sunday school, in clubs for boys and girls, in your Missionary Circle, or in a Vacation Bible School. Register voters in your town; be a hospital volunteer, or canvass your neighbors for charitable causes.

Deserve esteem by doing a good job somewhere!

George Macdonald advises those who are in darkness, having needs of their own, "Think of something thou oughtest to do, and go do it, if it be the sweeping of a room or a visit to a friend. Heed not thy feelings; do thy work."

Reach out for new interests. Become a more "interesting" person — not primarily so that others will be attracted to you but so that you will enjoy life — be an alive, enthusiastic, adventuring, growing person.

Read good, important, stimulating books. Learn to enjoy great music. Go in for sports, crafts, or other hobbies if you have time. Travel if you can.

If you are too restricted financially or time-wise to do some of these things, then savor life where you are — enjoy nature, people, your work, simple pleasures, your family, your church, and your Lord. Life never needs to be dull, not even if you're unpopular!

Because I was a single woman until I was forty, I must discuss the social problem you single people often face. Some of you want to be treated like any other adult — not segregated but integrated with your married peers. Others of you get fed up with listening to talk about babies, the P.T.A., and lawnmowers. You would rather share the company of other unmarried people — with the welcome possibility of finding a life partner.

Most churches make no provision for the needs of single adults, and I will make some suggestions in this direction in Chapter 9.

Right now I am concerned mainly with the loneliness of the single man or woman. Most of what this chapter has already said to the person with a social problem applies to you. Accept yourself (making all possible improvements!) and your situation before God, and then live your life to the full, without self-pity and without envying others. (Many of them envy you your freedom!)

Perhaps your biggest problem is that you would like to be married and have your own home and family. Some have wanted this so desperately that they have become twisted, pathetic hankerers, and some have had mental breakdowns or committed suicide.

The *only* full solution to your need is to commit yourself and your future to God, trusting Him to do with you what He will — giving you the life partner you long for, or giving you fulfilment outside of marriage.

As a career woman, I was too busy to spend much time worrying about getting married, but I did tell the Lord that if He had a man for me He could bring him around. I wasn't going to hunt for him. I believed that God was perfectly able to furnish me with a husband whenever He chose and, I used to add, even if there were only one man left on the earth and he was in Australia! And God did bring the right man into my life in His own time.

Are you willing to settle for God's plan and His timing for your life? Are you willing to live for His approval and trust Him to arrange your affairs? That is a decision you must make if you're to escape the frustrations many single people experience.

When you have made this basic commitment, you can meet or date a potential husband or wife with poise, quietly confident that God has His hand on the relationship and its outcome. You can be relaxed because you aren't terrified that some false move on your part might wreck the whole affair. And if there aren't any likely prospects on your horizon, you can live happily in real contentment (I did!) knowing that God isn't limited by what's in sight.

I used to say to myself that if I was going to be an old maid for the rest of my life, I was going to be as well preserved, up-to-date, and attractive a Christian woman as my natural endowments would allow. And that if the Lord should suddenly bring *the* man into my life, I wouldn't be anything less than my best when he arrived.

Be your best for whatever comes or doesn't come!

And please don't drop friends who get married just because you haven't made it to the altar. Men and women still value the friendship of the people they enjoyed before they were married. Go out to lunch together. If they invite you to their home, invite them back. Drop in to see them and compliment them on their new home.

It's silly to imagine that your now-married friend no longer has any use for you. Share his or her happiness sincerely and you may even get a glimmer of new respect for your own freedom setup!

Some lonely people let pets take the place of people in their lives. They lavish their love on these creatures and enjoy their company. A pet is sure to reciprocate your affection and doesn't involve you in the complications that mark some human relationships.

You take a bigger risk when you love a person than when you love a dog — but the rewards can be infinitely greater, too. So be ready to accept philosophically the problems and disappointments that may come from relating to people.

Keep your eyes on Jesus Christ, not on Christians whose friendship may be imperfect.

I remember a young man in our church youth group who was not a Christian but came to the meetings. One Sunday night after the youth meeting he became so disgusted with the quarreling and gossiping that was going on among these new Christian friends that he stalked off to the pool hall instead of staying for the evening service. It startled our church kids, but made them think!

No matter how short Christians may fall in their relation to you, stay with your Christian faith and with the Church of Jesus Christ. These are bigger than the imperfections of any individuals. Stay and help *make* the church the kind of fellowship that won't be disappointing.

Ask God to show you your real need in your poor social adjustment. Maybe your real need is for humility, or a cure for jealousy, or ability to accept life, to trust God and people, to learn that you are here not to be helped but to help others.

Remember that God understands your loneliness and your hunger for friends. Jesus was rejected by "his own,"[36] and He "is not One who cannot feel sympathy with our weaknesses."[37] His friends forsook Him in His hour of greatest need, but He will never desert you. "Be satisfied with what you have. For God has said, 'I will never leave you; I will never abandon you.' Let us be bold, then, and say, 'The Lord is my helper, I will not be afraid! What can man do to me?' "[38]

Paul wrote, of his hour of crisis, "No one stood by me . . . all deserted me . . . but the Lord stayed with me and gave me strength."[39] Paul's God is *your* God today. When you belong to Him, you are never alone.

Willing to Wait

When your personal relation to God is good and you have

committed your need for social acceptance to Him, be willing to wait for Him to work things out. Allow time for your own personal development, maturing, and change of character and attitudes. It may take time, too, for such improvements to register with others.

The waiting period can make room for the personal examination and soul-searching that you may desperately need. And a lapse of time may also be involved in God's solution to your situation — time for future events, people, and places to play a significant role in His plan for you. Don't expect an instantaneous solution to the problem you commit to God. He doesn't always work that way.

A college professor's wife told me of her lonely childhood. She lived on a farm way out in the country, too far from other people for her to have neighborhood friends. She traveled to and from school by bus, so could never participate in after-school activities. Her strict parents didn't put much stock in friends or fun, and so the years before she went to college were pretty bleak.

But at college a wonderful change took place! She found friends, was active in many extra-curricular activities, and married one of the most distinguished students on campus. She had had to wait, but her life blossomed in due season.

Now for a personal testimony. New in a large evangelical church, my husband and I were happily assimilated into a group of other also rather new people — upper middle class, prosperous, well-accepted folks. I remember the relief and delight it was to be part of this pleasant company.

After several years, however, we came to realize that we had been dropped by every one of these five or six couples. We didn't know why, so it was mystifying as well as disturbing. When I asked one of our erstwhile friends if we had offended anyone, she said, "Well, we knew you had been seeing a lot of Mrs. X" (a woman not in the group). When I asked if there was anything wrong with that, she said vaguely, "No . . ."

Although my husband and I recognized some areas where we might have displeased these friends, we had to settle for the unpleasant fact that they just didn't want us in their group. This bothered me much more than it did him, and for a long time. But one day over the dishpan I took the situation to the Lord, told Him I didn't know what to do about it, but that I determined not to think about it anymore. I admitted that we would like some new friends as replacements, and then promised Him that I was going to leave the whole business in His hands and trust Him to do whatever He chose about it.

I don't think I ever had a troubled thought about the situation again. God simply set me free of it. We enjoyed the assorted friends we still had and went on about our business.

After some months, new developments took place and we found ourselves drawn into a group of professional people who in special ways were our kind. They didn't drive Cadillacs, but they were independent, creative, stimulating, *idea* people — no better than our earlier friends, but different and much more right for us.

After many years of spiritual and intellectual sharing with these friends, we have moved nearly two thousand miles away, and the hardest part of leaving was separation from these friends God had so wonderfully brought into our lives.

Facing your problem squarely and turning it over to God can be one of the most exciting adventures of your life.

"Be patient, then, my brothers, until the Lord comes. See how the farmer is patient as he waits for his land to produce precious crops. . . . And you also must be patient! Keep your hopes high. . . . You have heard of Job's patience, and you know how the Lord provided for him in the end. For the Lord is full of mercy and compassion."[40]

9

THE CHURCH LOOKS AT THE PROBLEM

We have seen that in almost any church there are some people who don't feel accepted, loved, and cared for, who would like — and who need — to find personal friends among their Christian acquaintances.

Looking beyond what the individual church member can do to meet this need, what can the organized local church do about the situation?

First of all, let the church recognize that the need exists, instead of planning its ministry and program as though it didn't.

Some churches have justly been labeled social clubs. They put great emphasis on arranging things to do and go to, involving members in many activities. But somehow they fail to make adequate provision for the individual's need to feel loved and cared for. If a newcomer fits into the colorful social program of the church, well and good. One gets the impression that if he doesn't, he should go to some other church that may be more his speed!

Some churches exist primarily for outreach. They emphasize evangelism — bringing in the lost to be saved — even though the fellowship into which a new convert is deposited may fail to meet his personal need for acceptance, love, and friends. A person who has been "born again," these folk feel, should be so suddenly spiritual that he will be above such "carnal" needs and will now be preoccupied with the salvation of other lost souls.

In this kind of church also, new converts may fail to find the fellowship and loving concern they expect in the Church of Jesus Christ.

As we have seen, the first business of the church is to minister to the Christians within its walls, to meet their personal needs, lead them to growth and maturity, and equip them for the work of evangelism.

One neighbor said with bitterness, "The people in my church don't want to hear about our needs, and if they do know we're worried about something they never follow up or ask about it. My church has never done anything for me personally except supply me with offering envelopes!"

The church should be interested in the whole man (not just his soul or his wallet), and that includes his social and emotional lacks. An effective church will look beneath the veneer of smiles and handshakes to discover the real needs of its people and then set about meeting them.

Actually the loneliness and social insecurity of the *Outs* is only one face of the coin. The other is the pathetic failure of the *Ins* to show Christian love and grace toward all members of the Body of Christ. Until they come to grips with this responsibility they are (consciously or unconsciously) selfish, ignorant, uncaring, and guilty before God.

So this whole area of personal relationships in a church becomes an acutely tender and potentially infectious area that calls for the cleansing and healing touch of the love of Christ and of His people for one another. God will never be satisfied with the Church until these shortcomings are removed.

"God loved the Church and gave his life for it . . . in order to present the Church to himself, in all its beauty, pure and *faultless, and without spot or wrinkle, or any other imperfection.*"[1]

The leadership in most churches is made up largely of active, dominant, outgoing, well-liked people who by nature rise to the top, come to the front, and find themselves holding positions of responsibility and prominence. They may know little about this social problem in the church, and have experienced even less of it personally. They are *In* and may be quite unaware of the needs of people who haven't risen to the top, come to the fore, and received recognition.

Pastors too are usually poorly positioned to know anything about this lack in the church. They are leadership stuff and by their very position find themselves in the center of church life — rarely off on the fringes where the social *Outs* linger. Ministers are often so painfully aware of other situations in their churches — problems that are more directly related to themselves and the total church program — that they overlook the frustrating situations of their less-well-accepted parishioners.

I am a minister's daughter. The family in which I grew up was at the very core of church life. We three daughters had it made socially — among church people — just by virtue of being the preacher's kids. We were *In,* and perhaps that's the reason why (from this far distant view) I don't remember among the young people in our small church anything like the social discrimination, snobbishness, readiness to mock, humiliate and exclude, that is common in the youth groups of most churches today.

For fourteen years after graduate work I was assistant to the pastor in a large church and was surprised at the exclusiveness of the cliques I observed among the young people there.

One teen-ager came to my office to object to the fact that the *In* group excluded her. And a rather new woman in my Bible class told me plainly how resentful she felt that the *In* group among the church women had not accepted her.

It wasn't until — late in life — I got my wish to be married to a layman and just be an unofficial person, that I explored life apart from pastoral privilege. Then I learned what many inhabitants of the parsonage don't know — the tension and uncertainty and longing that goes with the normal experience of entering a new community and a new church relationship as an ordinary person with no official headstart. And I believe I now understand what many pastors and associated professionals are unable to sense — the lack of satisfying interpersonal relationships among many church members.

People are so embarrassed to admit their own feelings of rejection and loneliness that few pastors ever become aware of the situation. To be sure that some of these shepherds of the flock would read this book would be reward enough for the hard work involved in writing it. (If you'd like to alert *your* pastor, give him a copy!)

If you have any teaching ministry in your church, don't in your teaching gloss over the lovelessness and indifference you see there. Don't be afraid that talking about these unchristian attitudes will reflect on God and His church. The very existence of these conditions *already* reflects on both. The Bible speaks openly and severely about such unhealthy, sick attitudes, and supplies the prescription that heals.

If you're a teacher or preacher of God's truth, don't leave out this much-needed part of it. You can, without embarrassing individuals, relate to local situations what God has to say about a Christian's attitude toward himself and toward others. Be loving in the way you do it, but *do* it — and be as specific as a doctor is when he applies medication and bandage to a wound. This is the place where it hurts and where help is needed.

If frank discussion of social discrimination in your local situation might seem to be aimed at certain groups or individuals, perhaps you should schedule a chapter-by-chapter study of this book. That would provide safely hypothetical illustrations, obviously not designed by you to expose flaws among your members, but easily applicable to them.

The ten chapters would fit well into an adult Sunday School class elective or VBS course. A leader's study guide is available from your bookstore. Whatever you do, do something to help your people learn the crucial importance before God of right attitudes toward one another.

Unity in the Church?

Unity in a church — a sense of oneness — makes a large contribution to church growth and productiveness. The local church is properly concerned about unity, but may overlook the importance of each individual member's personal adjustment to others in the group. Without this there can be only a *veneer* of unity.

Some churches operate on the assumption that if every person in the congregation is given something to do (many small responsibilities are invented to make this possible), he will experience a satisfying relationship to his church. There is some truth in this, but it is utterly inadequate if mere busy-ness is expected to take the place of real fellowship of the *koinonia* kind.

When Christians in a local church understand *and practice* right attitudes in their relations with each other, the most solid foundation for unity has been laid. Then believers can forget themselves and serve each other, bound together by the practical loving that undertakes to meet each individual's need.

"Be humble, gentle, and patient always. Show your love by being helpful to one another. Do your best to preserve the unity which the Spirit gives, by the peace that binds you together."[2] Notice how closely humility, patience, and loving helpfulness are related to peace and unity (not necessarily unanimity!) in the church. They are God's antidote for snobbery, friction, conflict, harshness, and bitterness among His followers.

"When we are in union with Christ Jesus . . . what matters is faith that works through love."[3] To people who are not "in union with Christ," other things may matter much more — social status, power of office, personal convenience, elite friends, and exclusive, upper-crust doings.

Unity should be a major goal for a church, but it can be realized in its truest sense only among men and women who are regenerate — personally related to God in Christ — as well as thoroughly instructed as to His plan and power for Christian living.

Are the men and women, boys and girls, who are admitted to membership in your church genuinely related to Jesus Christ or are they just respectable church-goers? Does someone interview them before they are received into membership to find out whether or not they understand what it means to be a Christian? Overeagerness to add to the church rolls may be one reason why fellowship and unity in many churches are below par.

Oil and water don't mix. Genuine believers and mere

professing Christians may join the same organization — a local church — but they cannot become truly one except as each, by personal faith, is incorporated into that living organism, the Church of Christ. They can give money and render service and hold office in the church, but if they have never had a personal experience with Jesus Christ, His life is not in them, and their life perspective, goals, and resources are basically different. They can be "with" God's people, but they can't be "*one* with" them. And when such people infiltrate a church, even personal relationships among Christians may deteriorate.

So if a church wants a membership that is truly united, where Christian love can flourish and produce its beautiful fruit, it had better be more interested in quality than quantity when admitting individuals to membership.

New members who are new creatures in Christ at least have the potential for right relationships with others in the church, and with adequate teaching can become a well-adjusted, self-giving, cohesive part of the local church body.

Sense of Family

Even well-meant social arrangements may fail to provide a sense of close relationship to members of one's church. A lonely Christian put it this way: "There're those church coffee hours, you know, where fifty people go around balancing cups and cake, and never stopping long enough even to give their names. It's a great attempt but you can get lost in those things."[4]

A church needs to give its members a strong sense of family relationship — of belonging to each other as well as to the church, of being responsible for each other because they are brothers in Christ. We do for members of our families what we couldn't undertake to do for "outsiders." And it's this sense of family-in-Christ that makes it natural and delightful to give ourselves in practical, even costly ways, to meet each other's needs.

Listen to the Now Generation as they put to music their own strong sense of commitment to help one another:

The road is long,
With many a winding turn
That leads us to who knows where,
But I'm strong —
Strong enough to carry him:
He ain't heavy, he's my brother.

So on we go;
His welfare is my concern,
No burden is he to bear,
We'll get there . . .
If I'm laden at all
I'm laden with sadness
That everyone's heart
Isn't filled with the gladness
Of love for one another.

It's a long, long road
From which there is no return.
While we're on our way to there
Why not share?
And the load
Doesn't weigh me down at all;
He ain't heavy, he's my brother.*

As Christians in your church find a sense of relationship to each other in Christ they will experience a oneness that is unique, that will meet personal needs and will impress those on the outside with the reality of Christian love.

In the past we have sometimes become preoccupied with what an individual can do for the church (give money, teach a class, sing in the choir), but thinking churchmen today are shifting the emphasis and asking, What can the church do for the individual?

The church must not lose sight of its most essential ingredient — the individual believer. He desperately needs to be recognized and cherished as a person, not merely part of the congregational "lump."

Meeting this need for personhood and also for assimilation by the local church family demands a congregation that has been taught what real fellowship is and what personal relation-

---

*©1969 Harrison Music Corp.

ships among Christians ought to be. There will be little more than mere organizational unity in a church, and little satisfying fellowship among its members, until this teaching has taken place.

Spell It Out

If social problems among Christians are to be met, then, the church must recognize the situation and help its members to admit it and deal with it. But this may not happen unless the preaching and teaching staff of the church provides tell-it-like-it-is instruction.

Some impressive and scriptural sermons have been preached on love, but too often they are vague, general dissertations that slide with ease over the minds (and consciences!) of their hearers. Many preachers pride themselves that they present the principles of God's truth and trust the Holy Spirit to make the applications to the hearers. Experience shows that the Spirit is more likely to use an application that simply cannot be evaded.

The apostles — Paul and Peter and James and John — applied God's message to the most specific areas of the early Christians' everyday lives — incest and other sexual sins, uncontrolled tongues, partiality and discrimination, financial support of God's work. It is strange that preachers who find it important to be specific about one's duty to put a generous amount in the offering plate may think it unwise to be so specific about other areas of responsibility.

"All Scripture is inspired by God and is useful for . . . correcting faults and giving instruction for right living."[5] The goal of gospel teaching and preaching is not primarily to give out information but to change lives. Christ "gave himself for us, *to rescue us from all wickedness and make us a pure people* . . . eager to do good."[6]

The message of the Cross is not only forgiveness of sin and escape from judgment, but selfless living. "He died for all men so that those who live should *no longer live unto themselves,* but only for him who died and was raised to life for their sake."[7]

The same God-given truth that can save an unbeliever is also designed to lead a new Christian on, out of spiritual babyhood into healthy growth and maturity. Yet many a preacher is still serving up the "milk of the Word" long after he should be weaning his parishioners from the bottle to solid food — the "meat of the Word."[8]

Other preachers and their followers major in doctrinal preaching — "deep" Bible study. This is good so long as it is life-related — not merely a never-ending hunt for some new twist to truth that flatters the hearers' intellectual and spiritual sense of advance.

But as someone has said, there is "much trafficking in un-lived truth among evangelicals." These Christians are loyal to the authority of the Scriptures and the basic doctrines of the faith, but it is appalling to see how many of them fail to live the renewed life, especially in their relations with each other, that such great truths should set in motion.

Eternity magazine was praised by one of its readers for its "straightforward approach to race, poverty, the generation gap, sex, and a host of other imperative problems. We need," said the correspondent, "*more emphasis* on man's responsibility to man as part of his responsibility to God. We must learn to love people —not as we wish they were, but as they are."[9]

So spell it out! Help the *Ins* to understand how it feels to be *Out* and to reach out to those who are. Help the socially insecure to accept themselves, take their problems to God, and develop personal qualities and attitudes that will ease their dilemma.

Teach your people how to show their love for each other in specific, practical, personal ways (Chapters 5-8) — how to make newcomers in church feel at home; how to relate to sickness, bereavement, anxiety over lack of money, rebellious children, military duty, local or national emergencies; how to be a good listener when a brother needs to unload, how to use the Bible in encouraging Christians who need reinforcement.

A friend wanted me to share her experience with my readers. "Jack," she said of her husband, "wasn't interested in spiritual things. When we moved to the Northwest he always spoke of my church friends as *your* friends. But even though he put himself on the sidelines when he occasionally attended church with me, the people in that church just loved him into their fellowship. They never pressured him, but when we had problems we knew they cared — that if we ever needed help they would be there.

"Helping others was a large part of that fellowship," she explained. "There were all kinds of people in the church, but there was no distinction as to age or kind. There was real unity and each person was part of the group — even one coarse, gossipy, loudmouthed member who had been converted out of a life of immorality. She participated along with the rest, often with helpful touches. And I never heard that woman talked about behind her back.

"I see the people in that church as mature Christians," she added.

"But then," she went on ominously, "we moved to another part of the country and the church we attended was *so* different. The people were always there for Bible study and were enthusiastic about it. But once the sessions were over, what they'd heard didn't seem to overflow into their everyday living. There was little social mixing among the members and no fellowship in homes. We never felt we had any real personal friends there.

"They could always talk about 'the things of the Lord' but if you ever needed anything *else,* you felt you had no one to go to. Even though many knew that my husband was out of a job for a time, they paid no attention. It was so different from our former church that Jack just dropped out and I've never been able to get him interested again."

Attack the Problem

Don't overlook the particular social stresses to be found among your young people. Alert their teachers and youth sponsors to these needs. Take up such subjects as cliques, friendliness, and snobbishness. In a well-handled discussion, the participants themselves will often come up with sensible and even ingenious solutions.

Encourage your youth workers to do what they can, personally, to help individuals who are ignored or rejected, and to enlist the cooperation of others in the group who may be able to relieve the situation. Let the youth feel that Christians should be distinguished positively by what they *do* (e.g., kindness and compassion) not just negatively by things they don't do (those controversial taboos).

It's true that a poor vertical relationship underlies distressing horizontal relationships, and you have to deal with both.

Paul wrote about the person who "is all puffed up . . . by his human way of thinking, and *has stopped holding on to Christ,* who is the Head" and by whom "the whole body is nourished and held together . . . and grows as God wants it to grow."[10]

Keep Christ at the center of your message, for He is the Mainspring of Christian growth, love, and unity. Even young people (and many adults) who have entered into a personal relationship with Jesus Christ apparently don't realize the inconsistency of their wrong social attitudes and actions. But as Jesus Christ becomes more important to them they will be ready to respond to *His view* of their relations to each other when you *make it clear to them!*

Paul wasn't satisfied as long as his converts were lacking in right attitudes toward one another. "Do you feel kindness and compassion for one another?" he asked. "I urge you, then, *make me completely happy* by having the same thoughts, sharing the same love, and being one in soul and mind."[11]

And no Sunday school teacher, youth worker, or pastor should be satisfied until those he teaches have learned how to live in love with other Christians.

Paul was almost ecstatic over the growth in the believers at Thessalonica. "Your faith has made such strides, and (without any individual exceptions) your love towards each other has reached such proportions, that we actually boast about you in the churches of God."[12]

To see Christians experience this kind of development is one of the first responsibilities and greatest delights of a teaching ministry.

"We warn and teach everyone with all possible wisdom," said Pastor Paul, "in order to bring each one into God's presence as a mature individual in union with Christ. To get this done I toil and struggle, using the mighty strength that God supplies, *which is at work in me.*"[13]

Teacher, preacher, this responsibility and the labor involved are enormous. But your resources in Christ are adequate for the task! They are supernatural and God-given. Dare to set your goals high — reach the unchurched, yes, but also bring those already in the church to personal maturity in Christ. When fellowship, love, and caring are the order of the day on the inside, outsiders will begin to want to be a part of what they see taking place.

Why Go to Church?

"Going to church" seems to many to become increasingly less rewarding as time goes on. You hear folks say, "I'd get more out of reading my Bible at home!" (I've said it myself on occasion!) But of course the stay-at-homers don't always spend that time reading the Bible either!

One reason for this disenchantment with church-going was voiced by a friend who complained, "When I go to church I want something for my life right where I am *now,* and I'm not getting it!" We want the service and the preaching to relate to our present needs. We need encouragement, comfort, wisdom in decision-making, patience with our children, the ability to adapt to our husbands and wives, strength to endure long-lasting difficulties, bright hope for the future to relieve a distressing present. If we don't feel corrected or reinforced after going to church we go away feeling disappointed.

Preacher, and teacher, help your listeners (and yourselves, in the process) to understand what is supposed to happen when Christians come to church. "Let us be concerned with one another, to help one another to show love and to do good. Let us not give up the habit of *meeting together,* as some are doing. Instead, *let us encourage one another.*"[14]

We meet together with a group of Christians not only in order to receive instruction, but also to show loving concern, encourage and do good to one another. Let's hope that you who lead the congregation contribute to this end in your preaching and teaching and personal contacts, but when Christians meet together they should experience much more than what their leaders supply. The experience should be, as it was in the early Church, a warm exchange of love and helpfulness among all who are present.

Most church services today are not structured to allow for such interaction (more about that later), but Christians who have learned to love one another openly and practically can surround the services of their church with an aura of friendliness and mutual concern. People need this and hope for it when they come to church.

Paul was concerned that Pastor Titus should give proper attention to educating his congregation in the art of practical Christian loving. "I want to give special emphasis to these matters, so that those who believe in God may be concerned with giving their time to doing good works . . . to provide for real needs; they should not live useless lives."[15] Many Christians think they are too busy to spend time ministering to the needs of other Christians. Teach them that taking time for this is an essential part of God's plan for members of the church.

Some feel unqualified to help persons who have pressing needs. Be sure that you teach your people about the presence and power of the Holy Spirit who indwells every believer and stands ready to equip them for this sort of ministry.

Many Christians have only the vaguest ideas about the third Person of the Trinity. Make Him real to them as a Helper-alongside, a wise, powerful Companion who is active in all of a Christian's personal relationships.

One of the greatest needs of the contemporary church is for *leaders* who are not only well trained, experienced, and doctrinally sound, but who also know how to get along with people. Much of the effectiveness of a pastor, teacher, or other official in the church is determined by this qualification.

"There are two classes of men," says Sydney Harris; "those who are good with people and those who are good with ideas; and the main reason things are so badly run is that the men good with people usually have muddled minds, and the men good with ideas usually muddle their relations with people."[16]

This may be an oversimplification, but it speaks of the need shared by many fine idea men on the pastoral and teaching staffs of our churches: they don't know how to relate comfortably and meaningfully to each other or to the individuals in their churches. Unable to "get next" to them, pastors often know little of their people's real needs and so are unable, from the pulpit or any nearer vantage point, to help.

Plans are now underway for a series of seminars that will offer pastors and assistant pastors concrete help in learning how to get along with people. With such special training, their own ministry would be enriched and they could pass on to their members what they learn about building good personal relationships. These seminars will be offered under the auspices of the Advanced Institute for Pastoral Ministries under the direction of Larry Richards.

In order to win the liking of their pupils, Sunday school teachers need to learn what to *be,* as well as what and how to teach. It is important that the members of your class like you, because they may not learn much from your teaching unless they do!

Pastors and teachers, learn the names of your people. I have heard more than one parishioner complain that even after a year or more of faithful church attendance, "Pastor doesn't even know my name!" In many churches the pastor no longer visits his members in their homes. The church hires an associate to do this, and this greatly reduces the pastor's individual contacts.

When you meet one of your members at the door or impromptu somewhere, don't greet him with a witty remark: "Who let you out of jail so early in the day?" or — to a worshiper in a red dress — "I hope you don't meet a bull on the way home!" Such jesting will show how clever you are, but will leave the greeted one feeling flat if he can't come up with an equally clever response. Even if he does muster a smart retort, such an exchange effectively squelches any meaningful conversation.

A simple, sincere greeting accompanied by a smile, and using your parishioner's first name, will let him know you're

glad to see him and are open to anything he may be ready to
share with you.

Koinonia

Howard Snyder, in his excellent treatment of *The Fellowship of the Holy Spirit,* says that the superficial social fellowship experienced in many churches is something distinctly
less than *koinonia* and is "no more supernatural than the
weekly Kiwanis or Rotary Club meeting."[17]

Koinonia is that fellowship among believers "which the Holy
Spirit gives. It is precisely that experience of a deeper communion, or of a supernatural intercommunication, which perhaps every believer occasionally has felt in the presence of
other believers."[18] It is the Holy Spirit who makes this fellowship possible, but we can help or hinder by the degree to which
we consciously try to make touch with our fellow-Christians.
And some of us have never tried very hard.

Grant Howard notes that a process of giving and receiving is
involved in true *koinonia* — a responding of individuals to the
needs of others in the group.

But the Church does not make this easy. It has provided
ample opportunity (sometimes *too* "ample") for Christians to
gather together, but in meetings not structured for communication among individuals. Both the church building and the
order of service are designed for one-way communication —
pulpit to pew.[19]

Even a more informal prayer meeting or Sunday school
class is too often built on a "one-way," leader-to-group kind of
communication. "*Koinonia* appears and begins to grow only in
structures that allow and encourage [two-way] communication."[20]

Church structure, Snyder adds, must involve the element of
freedom. "Where the Spirit of the Lord is, there is freedom."[21]
This freedom and openness are possible only when there is informality and intimacy — "a sense of the unprogrammed . . .
the excitement of the unpredictable; a freedom from set
patterns and forms."

This is not an argument against "times of solemn corporate

worship in which God is honored with dignity and reverence. But in the midst of the dignity and reverence, many a lonely believer inwardly cries out for the warm, healing touch of *koinonia*. Believers need to know by experience that the Most High God is also the Most Nigh God."[22]

We were touched by some things we saw when we visited a charismatic group. Their meetings didn't follow the unchanging structure common to most churches. The music was not the traditional church music so many young people have rejected, but neither had they gone over to folk and rock. Their singing and praying — often with arms outstretched to God and hands open to receive[23] — visibly expressed their desire to experience a touch from the Lord.

Regardless of the merits of accompanying practices (speaking in tongues and healing), this unashamed admitting of personal need for God and of expectation to receive from Him had a peculiarly leveling effect. Black and white, rich and poor, unusually attractive, and painfully plain, in this unconventional, personal way, stood before God and before each other without pretense, unmasked, needy, eager, and full of praise for the Savior they worshiped.

The sense of openness in such a service helps those who participate to feel accepted, included, and even loved.

Some Christians find this experience of intimacy in worship that is more formal and restrained — the "proper" worship forms of other churches. But in such services any feeling of personal need or glowing enthusiasm for Jesus Christ is carefully contained and is quite invisible to fellow worshipers. And it is much easier, there, to feel separate from the others who sing and pray — isolated and perhaps lonely.

The hippies said simply, "Y'all come" to their "love-ins." The Jesus people — outside the conventional church — offer acceptance and caring and love to all who need, regardless of race or record, and without the trappings of traditional religion they present Jesus Christ simply — as Savior and Friend.

A Roman Catholic church in our neighborhood restructured its services to include, on occasion, what they called a Hootenanny Mass. Young people, sitting on the floor, and singing their own style of music accompanied by one of my neighbors on his guitar, were free — even during the observance of the Mass — to comment or ask questions of the priest.

Whatever we may think of these particular innovations, I believe that needed church renewal can come only as a church is ready to provide some kind of situation in which its people can share with each other the experience of *koinonia* — the fellowship of the Holy Spirit.

Elmer Towns reported that the ten largest Sunday schools in the country are found in "happy" churches that "attract kids like mad . . . a contagious friendliness, starting with the minister . . . that seems to inspire members."[24]

New Moves

Restructuring — or more truly *un*structuring — services at the Peninsula Bible Church in Palo Alto, California, has boosted evening service attendance from around 200 to nearly 1,000.

The pastor, Ray C. Stedman, gives this description: "The gathering is . . . a time for members of the body of Christ to fulfill the function of edifying one another in love . . . to 'bear one another's burdens' . . . to 'confess your faults one to another and pray for one another that you may be healed.'

"We determined to make a place for this ministry by wiping out the traditional structure of the evening service and using the time to invite a sharing of needs and gifts by the people. We began with the question, 'Where are you hurting *now,* right where you are?'

"Predictably it was slow getting started, but soon a climate of honest realism began to prevail. When that was noised abroad, without any particular invitation, youth began to appear — many longhaired, barefoot, and in bizarre dress. Our middle-class saints gulped at first but were determined to be genuinely Christian. They welcomed the young people and opened their hearts. The kids did likewise.

"The numbers increased by leaps and bounds, and it has been going on with no sign of let-up. Every service is different. Love, joy, and a sense of acceptance prevail so strongly that awed visitors frequently remark about a spiritual atmosphere they can almost scoop up in their hands. *Koinonia* has come!"[25]

Some Christians panic when new ways of presenting or experiencing old truth are suggested. They immediately become apprehensive, suspicious, fearful of any change in the conventional way of doing things.

It's true that some innovations have not been successful or have tended to overemphasize some phase of Christian doctrine or experience to the neglect of others. But as someone has said, "People are too worried about getting *off the track* when they should start worrying about getting *on the track.*" Every forward step involves some risk, but there's no progress without it. If we had always clung to old ways of doing things because they seemed safe, where would civilization be today?

So, then, I will dare to recommend small groups. Some evangelical Christians have condemned them — perhaps at least initially because they are widely used by the liberals. Or do people get a pleasant feeling of spiritual smugness because of their intensely conservative position?

New Testament *koinonia* was a sort of by-product, a serendipity of sharing. The early Christians shared meals and other material possessions, the joy of God's working among them, the fear and suffering of persecution. They shared other personal needs.

But there isn't much room for sharing in most churches today, especially in a larger church. Even in small churches there is usually little opportunity to share your real needs, and perhaps even then not much response toward meeting it. The traditional gathering together of believers is too structured for this, but smaller groups — especially in an informal home setting — make personal sharing possible.

Small groups constitute no peril if there is right balance between Bible study and sharing. A discussion leader, rather than a lecturing teacher, usually suits the informality of the session and encourages participation and freedom to voice needs.

Such home Bible study groups are not at all a substitute for the church — the coming together of the entire local body of believers. They are simply a happy, profitable part of it.

Many wary pastors make the mistake of disapproving small groups instead of sponsoring and supervising them. Others enthusiastically promote them because they realize their high potential in meeting the need of their people for meaningful personal relationships with other Christians.

Some churches are forming small groups in homes to replace or supplement the proverbial Sunday night service or the midweek prayer meeting, or they break up into small groups for sharing and prayer at church. Or neighborhood Bible classes meet in homes at different times during the week, providing for the needs of the church folks and at the same time drawing in others from the neighborhood who would not be reached otherwise.

As people in these smaller groups get to know and be open with each other they become free to share, and here — if not in larger church meetings — the individual church member comes to feel accepted, cared for, and loved. Experience sharing is kept in line by Bible study, and such sessions need not — and do not — degenerate into much-feared "orgies" of lurid confession.

It is important that the same people attend the same group consistently so they get to know and feel at ease with each other. Breaking up a joint session at church into random small groups that are made up of different individuals each time will not produce *koinonia*.

That's why it's so important for individuals who join a home Bible study to make a definite commitment to attend regularly, to give this meeting top priority on their calendar. The group will make little progress toward rewarding relationships if attendance is irregular.

The effectiveness of such groups far outweighs any hazards they may present. And any complications that do develop are no more serious than the loneliness and disappointment many Christians are finding in their churches. In the small group, if nowhere else, these folks come to feel personally related to a few Christians who know and care for one another.

When visitors who live in the area appear at a certain midwest church, two or three church couples in the visitors' approximate age bracket make a date with them for the next week. On the appointed evening they appear at the visitors' home bringing an entire meal with them — not only the food, but paper plates, napkins, silver, and whatever else is necessary. A meal is always the best kind of icebreaker, and the couples spend the evening together, giving the new people a taste of the warm fellowship that characterizes that church.

In another church new members are invited to the pastor's home for an evening — a few at a time — along with a few old-timers in the church. This helps the newcomers to know each other as well as meet some not-so-new people.

At one church, on the Sunday a group of new members is formally welcomed into the church, the deaconesses will have arranged an open house at each new member's home after that Sunday night's service. The refreshments are arranged by the deaconesses, and church families are assigned to the home where they are to go. There is no age segregation on this occasion, so young people and adults of different ages find themselves on the same welcoming committee.

Another church announced a number of coffees in homes one week, and asked the women in the church to go to the nearest home with the understanding that each would, before too long, invite those present to her own home for a coffee. Such small gatherings offer a good opportunity for people to become personally acquainted.

In one adult Sunday school class new members, who were briefly introduced when they first visited, may be interviewed later when they become regular members. Usually this is better than simply asking them to tell about themselves.

The interviewer (the teacher or some other qualified person) asks key questions that bring out what people would like to know about the newcomers: where they live; where they have lived in the past; their work; their children; how they happened to come to this church; their hobbies or other activities.

If the interviewer will talk with the new member privately before this public appearance, he will know how to elicit information that may be of unusual interest or with which others in the class may be able to identify.

Such interviews are probably better scheduled for a class

social gathering than for a Sunday session. If the group is large enough so everyone doesn't know everything about everyone else, interview some of the not-so-new members too, especially any who are involved in unusual careers or interesting recent experiences.

Another suggestion, from a friend who became a deaconess in her church: "A deaconess seems to hold a vague office where all the little unwanted jobs in the church are thrown at her. (I rebelled at making robes for the Junior Choir.) I got the deaconesses started inviting new members to their homes, along with some who were not new, for a get-acquainted evening.

"I liked to make it a simple casserole meal because I think there is something extra about sitting around a table. We found this most rewarding, got to know some people better than we would have otherwise, and made some lasting friends."

Another way to get people to know each other, and so be able to meet personal needs, is through the printed page. Our church in the midwest puts out a weekly news sheet called *The Spire.* It has local church news on one side and missionary news on the other. There is news of the sick, students, servicemen; engagements, marriages, births, deaths; softball teams, Sunday school picnics, youth activities; new members, lost-and-founds. This is *not* the Sunday church bulletin, and is mailed out to members (and adherents who request it) during the week.

This newsletter did more to make me feel an informed part of that sizeable congregation than anything else. It is not a substitute for personal contact, but lets people know current needs of the church family and so makes it possible for them to respond.

Another device that has been peculiarly effective in helping folks share their lives with each other was used in two adult classes in our church. One class called it the "Happy Cat" and the other the "Joy Kitty."

Each Sunday morning at the opening of the class session, members were invited to put something into a colorful feline bank to celebrate some event or development in their personal lives. In this way we learned about anniversaries, moves into new homes and the relief of having sold old ones, new babies, job promotions, recovery from illness, pleasant vacations, graduation of children and grandchildren, answers to prayer, and even the victory of a favorite team in national or intercollegiate sports.

The money so collected in our class was used to provide five dollars a month spending money for each of our church's missionary children who were in college — a most practical expression of love for young people who had little spare cash.

Planned Socials

Christians who have plenty of personal social life among themselves outside the church may feel little need for social activities in the church. But remember that some Christians have few such contacts on the outside with Christians they know, and this lack creates a real need for church-sponsored social get-togethers.

Too often, however, there is actually little getting acquainted at such church affairs. Those who plan either entertainment or game nights should keep clear among their goals the creating of situations in which those present learn names and come to know something of the persons behind the names.

If you use name tags print the names with a *broad* felt-tipped pen in letters as large as the space can contain. It's almost useless to write tags neatly with a ballpoint pen. No one can read them at a polite distance, so they fail to fulfill their purpose.

The officers of a group should understand that it's their business, from the moment guests begin to arrive, to introduce people, open conversations, and see that no one stands on the sidelines isolated and unincluded.

If the class is large, appoint a reception committee to help do this. Teachers, teach the members of your classes not to get in a huddle with their special friends but to reach out with genuine interest and concern to *every* member of the group. Developing this practice would transform the climate of almost any group of Christians.

I have learned one thing about taking a visitor to a church social. Don't count on everyone's rising to the occasion and making him welcome! Folks may not. To meet this situation, we would phone a few persons in our group and tell them ahead of time that we were bringing a visitor and would appreciate their help in letting him feel warmly received.

Too often, when you introduce visitors to another Christian, he acknowledges the introduction but makes no effort to show personal interest or carry on a conversation. To respond in such a situation should not be a chore but an opportunity to give yourself to others for Christ's sake — a warm, relaxed enjoyment of the human race. If *you* don't have that, ask God to give it to you.

One fairly large Sunday school class we attended came up with a delightful arrangement — fellowship dinners. On a Sunday well in advance, a sheet was passed around for the members to sign in one of three columns: as willing to be host and hostess to a small dinner party; as planning to attend one; or as not planning to come (since everyone not registered would be phoned).

The social chairman then assigned the guests to the homes that were willing to host a group on the basis of the number they could seat at their table. The names of the guests were given to the hostess, who telephoned them early in the week, inviting them to dinner Friday night. The hostess set the table and provided the meat, coffee, and rolls, but the guests brought everything else — salad, vegetables, and dessert. It was the easiest kind of entertaining.

I promised earlier to tell how we finally got acquainted with the couple who departed from Sunday morning class sessions in such an I'm-too-busy-to-talk-now manner.

The first time we hosted a fellowship dinner, the social chairman gave me an appalling list of three couples. One woman had offended me and I just didn't like her. One couple were so rigidly strict with their children that we wouldn't have chosen to know them better. The third name meant nothing to us. But I invited them by phone and they came!

When I answered the doorbell the third time, there was the couple I could never feel free to greet! Far from being haughty or unfriendly, they were warm, open, completely delightful people.

There was something unique about that evening. We were an odd assortment, but our common love for Christ and our coming together without any of us having chosen to be with the others proved to be a wonderful, intimate experience. I had planned some activities for the evening in case the conversation didn't go well after dinner, but my crutches weren't needed! And we felt a special closeness to those three couples for years after.

How much we need in our local churches to *know* the Christians who don't appeal to us, or who for some reason we may have foolishly written off!

In planning for church social affairs, don't always use the same few to prepare and serve the food, to put on a skit, or to help with the name-tag operation. Use some of the newer, shyer people. It will help them feel accepted and included.

Even though an experienced team of meal-fixers can operate at maximum efficiency in the church kitchen, lower your sights and let some other folks take part in the congenial performance. If you're making favors or decorations for a banquet, don't just get your own buddies to help. Invite some of the less socially-secure members of the group to participate.

I remember a charming and willing gal in our youth group who enlisted the aid of her boyfriend in preparing all the food for a large-scale cookout. She was willing to work long and hard, but she was selfish in not seeing this as an opportunity to help other fellows and girls feel part of the project.

Another girl who was social chairman made over 200 banquet favors single-handed, when others in the group, if they had been asked to help, would have been pleased, and have felt they were a functioning part of the whole.

The church has a special opportunity to show loving, personal caring when there is serious illness or death in one of its families. Arranging for meals, the care of small children, and trips to the doctor for someone who doesn't have a car are among the practical helps the church can offer.

But if you leave such help to close friends of the people involved, it may or may not get done. In a small church a chairman or committee or deaconesses can be responsible to organize the needed help — i.e., arrange who will bring meals *when,* who will take the patient to the doctor, etc. In a larger church the women's circles may be responsible for this ministry. Each circle in one church has a Sunshine Chairman who takes care of this service among members of that circle. Be sure, incidentally, that someone looks after needs in the pastor's family.

Singles, Widows, and Old Folks

What can the church do for single people? College young people feel out of touch with the church when they come home, and those who don't go to college and are unmarried usually prefer not to go into a young married couples' class. A college-career class should be a part of the program, meeting the need of these two groups.

One of the problems of these young singles groups is that when their members don't get married they stay on and on in the college and career class, with the result that after a while the younger singles won't come into the group.

Moral: Have a class for older single adults — and try to get them to come into it out of the younger class! Alternative: Start a new group of younger singles and leave the older ones to go on together.

Just be careful what you call these groups, so that eventually you don't have a "Young Adult" class of fifty-year-olds!

There are usually more single women than men, but don't let this lead you into the trap of a young business women's class. Most single people prefer to be in mixed groups, and it's amazing how many marriages originate in such a situation!

Since single people are not tied down by family responsibilities, many of them enjoy a fairly extensive program of active sports, weekend retreats, and other group activities.

If you don't have enough people in this category in your church, it may be possible to work out an organization for single Christian young people in a larger area, including several churches. Singles from one church are usually eager to meet singles from another.

An unmarried Christian friend in the middle-age bracket wrote this response to my query on the subject of the need for friends and fellowship among single Christians: "I've almost come to believe that even the church has little place for single older persons.

"Society in general is geared for family units, as it should be — and the church is an extension of this, I guess. It seems to me that all church activity is geared for the family. I imagine it's possible for a single older person really to feel a part of these activities, but it's certainly extremely difficult. I feel like a real misfit, frankly, although I know it isn't anyone's fault."

Widowed Christians also may find social adjustments difficult, feel lonely, left-out, in need of friends and social activities. I don't believe they are usually discriminated against by married Christians, but one widow had this shocking experience:

"My husband and I gave years of service to our church. Last year he died. At first the couples were very nice to me. Then, one day, a friend in the couples' Sunday school class said, 'You'll have to find other friends who do not have husbands. This class is for couples.'

"I have been very lonely. So has the 50-year-old single lady in our church who told me, 'I have been invited to wedding showers, weddings, baby showers, etc., through the years and have given and given. But there is no Sunday school class for me in our church. The socials are only for couples.'

"Now I ask you, isn't the church for *all* people — even for people with needs like ours? Why can't adult departments be for *all* adults? We need prayer — and help."[26]

Such shocking discrimination is a travesty on the name of Jesus Christ, and displays an utter lack of understanding of (or failure to practice) the clear teachings of the Word of God.

If the Sunday school doesn't come across for these folks, I

would suggest a home Bible study group for them and others in their situation.

Another needy and often dissatisfied group is the elderly people in a church — couples, widowed or singles. Their complaint? "They do everything for the young people, but nothing for us."

In confirmation of this situation, most churches don't have a Home Department — a ministry to particularly needy members who are not able to come to church regularly, who feel lonely, forgotten, and often resentful. Where Sunday school Home Departments *have* been instituted, they often disintegrate through disinterest and neglect on the part of those who carry on the ministry.

Loving and taking an interest in these elderly or handicapped Christians is one of the most productive ways of giving responsibility to members of the church who may not feel qualified to be teachers or leaders, but who can assume the responsibility of loving and keeping in touch with a few folks who need them desperately and who enjoy every visit and little kindness they supply.

Our church once had a 70-plus club, and went to great lengths to plan interesting activities suited to the limitations of its members. They had such good times folks began coming while still in their 60s!

What can your church do to meet the needs of those who attend its services — the need to know other Christians personally, to find friends, to share their real concerns — to tell where they're hurting *now?* Do people in your church understand what God means them to be to one another — listeners, encouragers, comforters, helpers? Do they *do* it?

And now ask yourself:

> What kind of church would my church be
> If everyone in it were just like me?

10

GOD LOOKS AT THE PROBLEM AND YOU

Where do *you* fit into the social problem picture in your church as God sees it?

Are you *In* — or enough so to be undisturbed?

Are you *Out* — or enough so to make you uneasy and dissatisfied?

Do you wish that in some group of Christians you could experience that special kind of fellowship called *koinonia*? Where could it happen in your world? What can you do to make it possible?

Have you been delivered from concern about yourself so that you're free to sense and minister to the needs of other Christians in the church to which you belong?

Are you using whatever gift God has given you to help them grow and become mature Christians? Do they find encouragement, comfort, friendship, and love in you?

What changes need to be made in you and in your church to help everyone there feel welcome, loved, and cared for?

How does *God* see you — as a meeter-of-needs in the lives of Christians around you?

When He looks at social problems among His people today, He sees them in the light of what He planned His Church and people to be.

He made it possible for believing sinners to be accepted into

His family — to come under His love and care. And His plan
was that they in turn would accept and love and care for each
other because of their common relationship to Christ.

God gave His Son to make this possible, and then He gave
the Holy Spirit to produce the family likeness in each of His
children — to replace the ugliness and childishness of sin with
the rightness and beauty of likeness to Jesus Christ.

And then He gave *again* — this time individual gifts to each
believer — not just to pastors and teachers. *"Each one of us
has been given a special gift,* in proportion to what Christ has
given. . . . He appointed some to be apostles, others to be . . .
pastors and teachers. He did this to prepare *all* God's people
for the work of Christian service, *to build up the body of Christ.*
And so we shall all . . . become mature men, . . . no longer
children . . . By speaking the truth in love, we must grow up in
every way to Christ, who is the Head. Under his control all
the different parts of the body fit together. . . . So *when each
separate part works as it should,* the whole body grows and
builds itself up through love."[1] What a plan!

Notice that in God's arrangements each Christian has a gift
to be used in building up other believers, helping them to become well-developed, mature Christians. Do you know what
your gift is? (Check Chapter 7.) Are you using it?

This is God's plan! And He hasn't abandoned it, even
though His people often fall short of it.

Does the Plan Work?

We are particularly concerned, in this book, with situations
in local groups of believers where God's plan for their relationships with each other has not been fully experienced. But let
me remind you that as God sees His Church today, there is
much to make Him glad.

He sees groups of believers in which there is no discrimination, where all kinds of people find welcome and love. He
sees individual Christians who have forgotten themselves as
they have become preoccupied with encouraging and caring
for the other members of their church family. Jesus' prayer
for the oneness of His people[2] has been answered in these

groups, and the reality of His own love has been demonstrated in their love for each other.

But how does God feel about Christians who have never been taught their role in the church, or who are too busy to know or meet the needs of other Christians? How does He react to thoughtless, uncaring church members who pick their way through the congregation, ignoring or snubbing people who need them and pursuing their buddies or people who may be of personal advantage to them?

God does not accept this as normal Christian conduct. Because of His plan for relationships between Christians, and what it cost Him to bring it into being, He can't be indifferent to such attitudes and actions. As we have seen, He reacts with indignation and anger.

"God will not show mercy when he judges the man who has not been merciful."[3] If you are guilty of unfriendliness, pride, selfishness, indifference, discriminating against some of God's children — confess it to Him and ask not only for forgiveness but for the personal renewal that will make it possible for you to fit into God's plan for His church and the people in it.

God is also aware of the grief and loneliness some Christians experience in relationships with other Christians. He is a God of compassion, sensitive to human need and suffering.

When His people Israel were ill-treated in Egypt, "in all their affliction he was afflicted."[4] He understands your problem even if people around you don't respond to it. And when God looks at your need He sees, perhaps better than you yourself do, the underlying causes of your problem. You, as well as those around you, may be at fault (Chapters 4, 6, 8). Have you failed to accept yourself and your life situation? To be your *best* self? To be friendly and outgoing?

God, who knows you and your problem completely, makes Himself available to you for the meeting of your need if you will bring it to Him. "He helps us in all our troubles, so that we are able to help those who have all kinds of troubles, using the same help that we ourselves have received from God."[5] When God meets a personal need in your life, He is equipping you to share and bear the burdens of others who face similar problems.

God's plan for His people was good to begin with, and He sees clearly where they fall short of His plan in today's world. But *He is still at work* in His Church, dealing with existing problems and producing — wherever He is given a chance — the warm, loving helpful personal relationships He intended.

"For God is always at work in you to make you willing and able to obey His own purpose."[6]

God cares about you and the group of believers to which you belong. He also cares about the world outside — a world that may never put any stock in Him or in His gospel unless they are impressed with the love of His people for one another. "If you have love for one another, then all will know that you are my disciples."[7]

So God is not indifferent when His children fall short of His high purposes in their interpersonal relationships. And when He sees that they walk together in love He is pleased and *He will bless.*

You and the Plan

Are you a thermometer Christian or a thermostat Christian? A thermometer simply registers a situation — how hot or cold it is. But a thermostat responds to the situation, *making* the temperature what it ought to be. One only registers, the other regulates.

Before you read this book, you belonged to one of three classes of people in relation to social problems among Christians: those who make things happen, those who watch what's happening, or those who don't know what's happening.

Now, if not before, you should be aware of the social problems among Christians. And from now on you will belong to one of three groups: those who *know* about it, those who *talk* about it, or those who *do* something about it. Even though you're only a committee of one in your church, you can set the ball rolling and help meet needs in the lives of your brothers and sisters in Christ.

If you happen to be among those who have a personal need

for acceptance and friends, face your problem honestly and optimistically. Commit it to God, revel in the fact that He accepts you as you are, that His friendship and love never fail, and that He will work in the area of your human relationships if you will depend on Him.

"The only way to be really independent of the opinions, criticisms, and demands of others is to put oneself into dependence upon God."[8]

"If you want favor with both God and man . . . then trust the Lord completely; don't ever trust yourself. In everything you do, put God first, and he will direct you and crown your efforts with success. Don't be conceited, sure of your own wisdom. Instead, trust and reverence the Lord."[9]

Burkhart, writing about *The Person You Can Be,* says, "Some mistakenly believe that they can become 'the person they can be' on their own; others feel that God in His infinite grace will do it for them. Both are wrong. No person can become whole alone. I have discovered that I cannot have a garden without God; God has chosen not to have one without me, but together we can have a great garden."[10]

Since God is in the business of your life, live expectantly, eagerly, confidently, patiently, even though now you lack the acceptance and friends you long for. Others have to accept and go on with a variety of handicaps, physical or financial: "awful" parents, partners, neighbors, or bosses. But with God in the picture, life for these handicapped ones and for you can be good — rich and satisfying and rewarding.

One thing is even more exciting and wonderful than entering into personal relationship with Christ. That is living, from then on, a life that is centered in Him, devoted to Him, and involved completely in His purposes.

It's like getting married. It's wonderful at last to be officially joined to the one you love "from this day forward," completely and "until death do us part." But if it's a good marriage, there is something more wonderful than "getting tied." That is living together in love, day after day, month after month, and year after year — pleasing each other, meeting each other's needs, and sharing and fulfilling plans together.

Every true believer is a member of the Church universal which is seen in Scripture as the bride of Christ.[11] In this relationship, how fully are you and the Christians around you involved in fulfilling His plans, sharing His interests, pleasing Him?

Even if you have friends in abundance, you still need, as every Christian does, a close personal relationship with God. "As the deer pants for water, so I long for you, O God. I thirst for God, for the living God."[12] Let His friendship and approval always be more important to you than the approval of anyone else.

Some people foolishly become unpopular with God in order to be more popular with men. "You like to have praise from one another, but you do not try to win praise from the only God."[13] And when some Jewish leaders kept secret their belief in Jesus, John commented, "They loved the approval of men rather than the approval of God."[14]

Portrait of a Christian

When Paul had to make a choice of goals, he wrote, "Does this sound as if I am trying to win *men's* approval? No! I want *God's* approval! Am I trying to be popular with men? If I were still trying to do so, I would not be a servant of Christ."[15]

"Try to learn what pleases the Lord," he wrote the Ephesians. "Pay close attention to how you live. Don't live like ignorant men, but like wise men. Make good use of every opportunity you get, because these are bad days. Don't be fools, then, but *try to find out what the Lord wants you to be.*"[16]

Someone has called Romans 12 "The Portrait of a Christian." Take a look at yourself in this mirror "to learn what God wants you to be":

"We are to use our different gifts in accordance with the grace that God has given us. If our gift is to preach God's message, we must do it. . . . If it is to serve, we must serve. If it is to teach, we must teach. If it is to encourage others, we must do so. Whoever shares what he has with others must do it generously; whoever has authority must work hard; whoever shows kindness to others must do it cheerfully. "Love must be completely sincere. Hate what is evil, hold on to what is good. Love one another warmly as brothers in Christ, and be eager to show respect for one another. Work hard and do not be lazy. Serve the Lord with a heart full of devotion. Let your hope keep you joyful, be patient in your troubles, and pray at all times. Share your belongings with your needy brothers, and open your homes to strangers.

"Ask God to bless those who persecute you; yes, ask Him to bless, not to curse. Rejoice with those who rejoice, weep with those who weep. Show the same spirit toward all alike. Do not be proud, but accept humble duties. Do not think of yourselves as wise.

"If someone does evil to you, do not pay him back with evil. Try to do what all men consider to be good. Do everything possible on your part to live at peace with all men. Never take revenge, my friends, but instead let God's wrath do it. . . .

"If your enemy is hungry, feed him; if he is thirsty, give him drink; for by doing this you will heap coals on his head. Do not let evil defeat you; instead, conquer evil with good."[17]

Is this your pattern for living? As one whom God has redeemed at infinite cost from the guilt and penalty of sin, just whom are you living for — yourself or Jesus Christ? Are you ready to offer to God the sacrifices that please Him?

"Let us then always offer praise to God as our sacrifice through Jesus Christ. . . . Do not forget to *do good* and to *help one another,* for *these are the sacrifices that please God.*"[18]

If pleasing God is what you're most concerned about, you can live with wrong attitudes on the part of others when you have to. Your own attitude toward individuals or toward a group will be determined not by their attitude toward you but by your attitude toward Christ. You will do and be what pleases Him, whether they respond warmly or not, whether or not they cooperate or appreciate you.

This is the best kind of freedom — freedom from self with all its demands and self-centered reactions. Catherine Marshall paints the contrast: "The egocentric personality is concerned about other people's opinions of self; craves admiration and popularity . . . loves those who love him. The God-centered personality is increasingly free from the necessity for the approval or praise of others . . . can love the unlovely; has a feeling of oneness in God toward all humanity."[19]

Have you made that glorious transition? Even in my late years I am still discovering the goodness and excitement of an increasing measure of such freedom. Don't miss it! Let God teach you the art of loving and self-giving, and then *keep on loving* more and more.

"There is no need to write you about love for your fellow believers," Paul wrote happily to the young church at Thessalonica, "for you yourselves have been taught by God how you should love one another. And *you have behaved* in this way toward all the brothers in all Macedonia. So we beg you, brothers, to *do even more.*"[20]

Extra Dividends

When you please God by serving others, you are giving happiness, not trying to get it. But strangely enough, you yourself find what you aren't looking for — happiness — the joy of pleasing God, of meeting human need, of making Christianity believable to an unbelieving world.

After Jesus had washed His disciples' feet He said, "I am your Lord and teacher, and I have just washed your feet. You then should wash each other's feet . . . do just what I have done for you . . . Now you know this truth; *happy you will be if you put it into practice!*"[21] When you love and help others in practical, humble ways, you will get — as well as give — happiness.

You may also acquire friends as a result, but that should never be the goal of your loving. Give yourself freely without demanding return on your investment, and the dividends will come.

Loneliness will go. Kenneth Strachan describes the close relation between this kind of self-giving and the escape from loneliness:

"Loneliness arises not from isolation of spirit. . . . Loneliness results in part from the illusion sinful man indulges that he can live with other persons without committing himself to share in their concerns, or entering into a responsible interdependence.

"The walls between persons which are created by our culture can only be scaled by the kind of concerned love that does care and share. The deepest needs in human life are met by love and acceptance. . . . Unless I give myself to others (and not necessarily to the kind of people I instinctively like or would want to choose for my friends) then, regardless of my physical surroundings, and no matter how many people are in the house I live in, I'm doomed to experience the frightfulness and frustration of loneliness.

"But as long as there are human beings to whom I can relate in some sort of out-going and self-giving, and as long as there is a loved and loving One who seeks to meet me in the fellowship of the 'hidden room,' I need never know loneliness, though in His will I may often know solitude."[22]

Loving others for Christ's sake will please Him, make you happy, and keep you from loneliness. And whether others appreciate it or not, *God will not overlook it.*

"Keep busy always in your work for the Lord, since you know that nothing you do in the Lord's service is ever without value."[23]

"When you help the poor you are lending to the Lord — and he pays wonderful interest on your loan."[24]

"God is not unfair. He will not forget the work you did, nor the love you showed for him in the help you gave and still give your fellow Christians."[25]

NOTES

Chapter 1

1 James Johnson, *Christian Life,* (November 1969), p. 54.
2 A. B. Hollinshead, *Elmtown's Youth* (New York: John Wiley and Sons, Inc., 1949), p. 246.
3 Proverbs 26:18, 19*
4 Vance Packard, *The Status Seekers* (New York: David McKay, Inc., 1959), p. 289.

Chapter 2

1 James 2:15, 16**
2 Roy A. Burkhart, *The Person You Can Be* (New York: Harper and Row, 1962), p. 24.
3 Vance Packard, *op. cit.,* pp. 286-288.
4 Matthew 20:20-28.
5 Margaret Mead, *And Keep Your Powder Dry* (New York: William Morrow and Co., 1942), p. 68.
6 Vance Packard, *op. cit.,* p. 226.
7 Lichtenberg, 200 years ago!
8 R. K. Merton, *Social Theory and Social Structure* (Glencoe, Ill., 1963).
9 Margaret Mead, *op. cit.,* p. 69.
10 Morgan and King, *Introduction to Psychology* (New York: McGraw-Hill Book Co.).
11 *Ibid.,* p. 467.
12 Keith Miller, *The Taste of New Wine* (Waco, Texas: Word Books, 1965), p. 22.

---

* References to Proverbs are from *The Living Bible* (Wheaton, Ill.: Tyndale House Publishers, 1971).

** Unless otherwise indicated, New Testament references are to *Today's English Version of the New Testament,* Copyright © American Bible Society, 1966, 1971, and are used by permission.

Chapter 3

1   John 17
2   1 John 1:3
3   James 2:5
4   1 Corinthians 1:26-28
5   Acts 6:7
6   Acts 17:12
7   Galatians 3:28
8   Ephesians 2:19
9   Acts 2:47
10 Howard A. Snyder, "The Fellowship of the Holy Spirit," *Christianity Today,* (November 6, 1970), p. 4.
11 James 1:1
12 Ephesians 3:18
13 Romans 3:22
14 Jude 3
15 Romans 15:7
16 1 Corinthians 3:3, 4
17 James 2:1-9

Chapter 4

1   Ephesians 4:22-24
2   F. Alexander Magoun, *Living a Happy Life* (New York: Harper and Brothers, 1960), pp. 28, 29.
3   Larry Richards, *Are You for Real* (Chicago: Moody Press, 1968), p. 14.
4   Paul Tournier, *Escape from Loneliness* (Philadelphia: Westminster Press, 1948), pp. 133-136.
5   1 Peter 5:7
6   *His* Magazine, (June 1967), p. 19; parentheses added.
7   Proverbs 26:22, 20
8   Proverbs 26:12
9   Proverbs 29:20
10 Horst Symanowski
11 Philippians 4:5
12 1 Corinthians 13:4
13 Ephesians 4:29
14 Proverbs 19:22
15 Proverbs 19:11
16 Psalm 139:23, 24

Chapter 5

1   Ephesians 4:25

2   1 Corinthians 12:12-27
3   John 3:16
4   *Decision,* (July, 1969), p. 15.
5   John 14:15
6   John 15:12
7   1 John 4:20, 21
8   Ephesians 3:18
9   Hebrews 13:1
10 1 Corinthians 13:7
11 1 Peter 2:15, 17
12 1 John 4:7, 12
13 1 John 3:14
14 1 John 4:8
15 1 John 4:9
16 Matthew 5:43-47
17 Romans 1:14
18 Yvonne Vinkemulder, "Exclusive," *His Magazine* (April 1970), p. 8.
19 Vance Packard, *op. cit.,* p. 19.
20 "We've Lost the Art of Friendship," *Saturday Evening Post* (August 26, 1967), p. 10.
21 A. D. Schanz, "Was This Your Church?" *Power for Living* (August 24, 1969), p. 3.
22 Proverbs 13:7
23 2 Corinthians 6:11-13
24 Romans 2:11
25 Acts 10:34
26 Mark 3:13, 14
27 Mark 4:34
28 John 11:3, 5
29 Ignace Lepp, *The Ways of Friendship* (New York: The Macmillan Co., 1966), p. 28.
30 James 1:17
31 "How to Succeed with Young People," *Eternity,* (November 1969), p. 24.
32 Tyndale House Publishers, Wheaton, Ill.
33 Proverbs 27:19
34 Proverbs 18:24
35 Proverbs 17:9
36 Proverbs 18:19
37 Proverbs 27:14
38 Proverbs 25:17
39 Proverbs 27:10
40 Proverbs 27:6
41 Proverbs 25:25

Chapter 6

1 Author unknown
2 1 Corinthians 1:26
3 Larry Richards, "Is God Necessary?" *Moody Monthly* (November 1969), p. 95.
4 Keith Miller, *Habitation of Dragons* (Waco, Texas: Word Books, 1970), p. 167.
5 Matthew 20:16
6 1 Corinthians 13:4
7 Proverbs 27:4
8 Proverbs 28:21
9 Proverbs 14:20
10 1 Corinthians 4:6, 7
11 1 Corinthians 1:27-29
12 Romans 12:3
13 Proverbs 16:18
14 Proverbs 16:5
15 Proverbs 6:16-19
16 Proverbs 8:13
17 Philippians 2:3
18 Proverbs 16:19
19 G. P. Smith, *The Tozer Pulpit* (Harrisburg: Christian Publications, Inc.)
20 Philippians 4:2 (Phillips)
21 Romans 14; 1 Corinthians 8
22 Luke 12:48
23 Philippians 3:7, 8
24 Ephesians 2:11-13
25 1 Timothy 6:17, 18
26 Motto in a bicycle shop.

Chapter 7

1 Matthew 20:25-28
2 Philippians 2:19-21
3 Philippians 2:4-11
4 John 13:4, 5, 12-16
5 Luke 22:41-44
6 Reuell Howe, *The Creative Years* (New York: The Seabury Press, 1967), p. 21.
7 1 Thessalonians 2:8
8 Roy A. Burkhart, *op. cit.*, p. 23.
9 Jacob Loewen, "The Way of Self-exposure," *His Magazine* (November 1966), p. 1.
10 Luke 10:30-37
11 2 Timothy 1:16

12 Mark 6:45-51
13 1 John 3:18
14 Ephesians 4:2
15 Ephesians 2:8-10
16 Titus 2:14
17 Author unknown
18 Donald E. Smith, "The Healing Touch of Attention," *Guideposts* (April 1969).
19 Romans 12:15
20 1 Corinthians 12:26
21 1 Corinthians 14:3
22 Proverbs 12:25
23 Acts 14:22
24 Romans 14:19
25 Hebrews 7:1
26 1 Thessalonians 2:7-12
27 Ignace Lepp, *op. cit.,* p. 12.
28 Matthew 5:44
29 "That Christian Glow," *Decision* (June 1962), p. 9.
30 Philippians 4:1, cf. 1 Thessalonians 2:17-20
31 Ephesians 6:18, 19
32 1 Corinthians 12:28
33 1 Corinthians 16:18
34 1 Peter 4:8, 9
35 Matthew 10:40, 41
36 Matthew 25:31-40
37 Luke 14:12-14
38 3 John 6-8
39 Hebrews 13:2
40 1 Timothy 5:10
41 1 Timothy 3:2
42 Titus 1:8
43 Proverbs 11:17
44 "How to Deal with Tensions," *Reader's Digest* (March 1969), p. 90.
45 Byron Frederick, *Ohio Grange Monthly.*

Chapter 8

1 Psalm 51:10
2 Galatians 2:20
3 Colossians 3:1-4
4 Colossians 2:20—3:2
5 Luke 22:42
6 Author unknown
7 Ignace Lepp, *op. cit.,* p. 36.
8 Proverbs 10:17

9 Proverbs 23:12
10 Proverbs 15:31, 32
11 Paul Tournier, *op. cit.*
12 Luke 9:51-56
13 Roy A. Burkhart, *op. cit.*, p. 102.
14 Proverbs 28:3
15 Romans 2:1
16 Proverbs 19:3
17 Donald E. Smith, *op. cit.*
18 Ecclesiastes 10:12
19 Proverbs 18:6, 7
20 Proverbs 15:23
21 Proverbs 10:19
22 Ecclesiastes 5:3
23 Colossians 4:6 (RSV)
24 Proverbs 25:11 (AV)
25 Luke 19:1-10
26 2 Timothy 1:7 (The Living Bible)
27 Philippians 4:10-13
28 F. Alexander Magoun, *op. cit.*, p. 41.
29 Reuell Howe, *op. cit.*, p. 25.
30 Paul Tournier, *op. cit.*, pp. 135, 136.
31 Philippians 4:6, 7
32 Jacob Loewen, *op. cit.*, p. 24.
33 George S. Stevenson, *How to Deal with Tensions*, (New York: National Association for Mental Health, 1957).
34 Billy Graham, "Loneliness: How It Can Be Cured," *Reader's Digest* (October 1969), p. 137.
35 Syndicated newspaper column.
36 John 1:11
37 Hebrews 4:15
38 Hebrews 13:5, 6
39 2 Timothy 4:16, 17
40 James 5:7-11

Chapter 9

1 Ephesians 5:25-27
2 Ephesians 4:2, 3
3 Galatians 5:6
4 James Johnson, *op. cit.*, p. 54.
5 2 Timothy 3:16
6 Titus 2:14
7 2 Corinthians 5:15
8 1 Corinthians 3:2
9 *Eternity* (November 1969), p 7.

10 Colossians 2:18, 19
11 Philippians 2:1
12 2 Thessalonians 1:3, 4
13 Colossians 1:28
14 Hebrews 10:24, 25
15 Titus 3:8, 14
16 Syd Harris, *Chicago Daily News* (August 28, 1970).
17 Howard Snyder, *op. cit.,* p. 5.
18 *Ibid.,* p. 6.
19 *Ibid.*
20 *Ibid.*
21 2 Corinthians 3:17
22 Snyder, *op. cit.,* p. 7.
23 1 Timothy 2:8
24 Elmer Towns, *Christian Life* (October 1969), p. 44.
25 Ray C. Stedman, *Christianity Today* (May 21, 1971), p. 39.
26 *Christian Life* (January 1970), p. 9.

Chapter 10

1 Ephesians 4:7-16
2 John 17
3 James 2:13
4 Isaiah 63:9
5 2 Corinthians 1:3, 4
6 Philippians 2:13
7 John 13:35
8 Paul Tournier, *op. cit.,* p. 64.
9 Proverbs 3:5-7
10 Roy A. Burkhart, *op. cit.,* p. xv.
11 Ephesians 5:22, 23
12 Psalm 42:1, 2
13 John 12:43
14 *Ibid.*
15 Galatians 1:10
16 Ephesians 5:10, 15, 16
17 Romans 12:6-21
18 Hebrews 13:15, 16
19 Catherine Marshall, *Beyond Ourselves* (New York: McGraw-Hill Book Co., 1961), p. 191.
20 1 Thessalonians 4:9, 10
21 John 13:13-17
22 R. Kenneth Strachan, *Who Shall Ascend* (New York: Harper and Rowe, 1968), p. 164.
23 1 Corinthians 15:58
24 Proverbs 19:17
25 Hebrews 6:10